Killer

of the Christ

According to the Bible

By

Marco Liang

Contributor: Amanda Liang
Editors: Rebecca Liang
Kevin Liang

—

Killer of the Christ

According to the Bible

—

Copyright © 2019, by Marco Liang

ISBN 978-1-7341090-0-9

All Rights Reserved

Contents

Preface - - - - - - - - - 7

Chapter 1
> *Killer of the Christ*
> *According to the Bible - - - 13*

Chapter 2
> *The Tares - - - - - - - - 35*

Chapter 3
> *Don't Eat, Don't Touch - - - 57*

Chapter 4
> *The Conspiracy - - - - - 89*

Chapter 5
> *The Day of Vengeance - - - 121*

Preface

The purpose of this book is to present an important set of truths that have always been in the Bible. This book is not intended to teach, but rather to share carefully gathered research used to discover the truth about the real killer of the Christ, including the events that led to it, and the events to come as a consequence/result of it.

According to the Bible, by the killer's own admission, they are the children of the killer of the prophets;

> **And say, If we had been in the days of our fathers, we would not have been partakers with them in the blood of the prophets.** (Matt.23:30)
>
> **Wherefore ye be witnesses unto yourselves, that ye are the children of them which killed the prophets.** (Matt.23:31)

By their own words, they also took full responsibility for the precious blood of the Lord Jesus Christ;

> "… and said, His blood *be* on us, and on our children." (Matt.27:25)

In light of these scriptures, perhaps we can see through God's Word to precisely trace the Killer of the Christ with confidence. It is not only because Jesus Christ identified His killer's true identity and taught about them in a parable, but it has also been prophesied from the foundation of the world — as it is all written in the Bible.

So this is great news! Because there is really nothing mysterious about it, and as it is written, so it shall be …

Let us begin the research of the Bible and see the truth behind the scriptures. May God open our spiritual eyes and ears, that we may see and understand the truth.

Naturally, we might ask the same question as Pontius Pilate asked Jesus nearly two thousand years ago, "What is truth?" (John 18:38). Let us find the answer to that question from Jesus Christ Himself.

When Jesus was praying to the Father for those that were chosen before the creation of this present world (John 17:9–19) and for those that would believe in Jesus through them (John 17:20–26), Christ said, "Sanctify them through thy truth: thy word is truth." (John 17:17) So the answer to Pilate's question is that the Word of God *is* the truth.

As study supplements to the Bible for search of the "Truth," we will be using the *King James Version (KJV)* and *The New Strong's Exhaustive Concordance of the Bible*. Let God's Word do the teaching and explaining, as we piece together the puzzle of the killer of the Christ. It is what God says that is important rather someone else's opinion or interpretation, which might only lead to confusion. After putting the scriptures together that lead to the killer, it is still, of course, up to the reader to form his or her own conclusion of the real killer of the Messiah, Jesus the Christ.

The Bible as a whole, is like a puzzle. It needs patience to piece all the pieces together to realize God's plan for us to understand why we are here, where we came from, and where we are going after our flesh body expires.

God said, "My people are destroyed for lack of knowledge" (Hosea 4:6). So let us continue searching for truth from God's Word, for all knowledge and wisdom comes from God.

As we gain knowledge of the truth, our faith in Almighty God will naturally grow. We have faith because we know and understand the words of God which is the "Truth." To build faith in our Heavenly Father we need to understand His Word, the Bible. The more we learn and understand the truth, the stronger our faith will grow. It is absolutely not needed to blindly believe in something that we don't quite understand; it is the accumulation of knowledge of the truth that truly builds up someone's faith in God.

Killer of the Christ will be revisiting popular parables such as: The Parable of the Sower, the Parable of the Tares of the Field (ch.2), and the Parable of the Ten Virgins (ch.3). You may have heard these parables (many times) before, or even know and understand them, but for some it's still a puzzle putting the lessons together to see the bigger picture. It may be the unawareness of one or two simple truths from the word of God that is missing from the picture. It is common that the answer to a question leads to more questions, and unfortunately, it leads to a lot of confusion, causing overwhelm or disbelief in the Bible — and sometimes even apostasy.

In regards to the prophesized second advent, the Lord Jesus Christ is not slow with what He has promised, but rather, He is being patient for our sake. Because His desire (as far as it depends on us) is for everyone to have the Knowledge of God, and to learn and understand the word of God and thus to repent for salvation before He returns. Consider that the patience of the Lord Jesus Christ means salvation:

> **For I desired mercy, and not sacrifice; and the knowledge of God more than burnt offerings.** (Hosea 6:6)
>
> **The Lord is not slack concerning his promise, as some men count slackness; but is longsuffering to us-ward, not willing that any should perish, but that all should come to repentance.** (2Peter 3:9)
>
> **And account *that* the longsuffering of our Lord *is* salvation;** (2Peter 3:15)

When the disciples asked Jesus privately about the Second Advent, the very first thing Christ said was, "Take heed that no man deceive you." (Matt.24:4) We should take that warning with great caution and not to let anyone deceive us, not to let any false prophets, nor the antichrist deceive us before the second coming of the true Jesus the Christ. Only those who overcome the deception will have part of the first resurrection (Rev.20:5) and be part of the kingdom of heaven.

For those that are deceived, they will not take part in the first resurrection. They will be spiritually dead and remain spiritually dead until the end of the millennium year. It is then that the great white throne judgment will take place. They will either participate in the second resurrection or participate in the second death — the death of the soul:

"**But the rest of the** (*spiritually*) **dead lived not again until the thousand years were finished. This is the first resurrection.**" (Rev.20:5)

In his first letter to the Corinthians, Apostle Paul described a secret truth about the second coming of the Lord Jesus Christ:

> **Behold, I shew you a mystery; We shall not all sleep, but we shall all be changed,** (1Cor.15:51)
>
> **In a moment, in the twinkling of an eye, at the last trump: for the trumpet shall sound, and the dead shall be raised incorruptible, and we shall be changed.** (1Cor.15:52)
>
> **For this corruptible must put on incorruption, and this mortal** *must* **put on immortality.** (1Cor.15:53)

In other words, when the last (the seventh) trump sounds (which is also when the true Christ returns), all the living people on earth will transform from a flesh body into a spiritual body i.e., from terrestrial to celestial bodies. At the same time, for the spiritually dead, their soul will remain mortal (still liable to die) — that is the second death. However, for those that overcome the deception of the Antichrist, their soul will no longer be mortal but will change to an immortal (deathless) soul.

Before the second advent transpires, the overcomers of deception in this world age will gain immortality for their mortal soul. This means everlasting life of the soul through the Lord Jesus Christ.

The immortality of our soul, especially in this generation, will truly depend on how much knowledge of God we have, which is needed to prevent deception in this world age. With knowledge of the truth, we will be able to recognize the differences between the false Christ and the true Christ. If it is God's will, may this book provide the reader answers about the truth, guide the reader to hear the word of God with understanding, and to prepare the reader for the second coming of Jesus Christ.

"He that hath an ear, let him hear what the Spirit saith unto the churches; He that overcometh shall not be hurt of the second death." (Rev.2:11)

Chapter 1
Killer of the Christ
According to the Bible

> I will open my mouth in a parable: I will utter dark sayings (*a puzzle or a riddle*) of old: (Psalm 78:2)

The word of God always comes to pass as it is written. Jesus Christ often spoke of parables in the New Testament, which is exactly how He taught and revealed the truth of God's Word.

> And the disciples came, and said unto him, Why speakest thou unto them in parables? (Matt.13:10)
>
> He answered and said unto them, Because it is given unto you to know the mysteries of the kingdom of heaven, but to them it is not given. (Matt.13:11)

The true identity of the killer of the Christ is one of the mysteries in the Bible. To those that can understand the parables, to those that can see and hear the words of God with understanding, Jesus said they are blessed because it was not meant for everyone to hear with understanding.

> But blessed *are* your eyes, for they see: and your ears, for they hear. (Matt.13:16)
>
> For verily I say unto you, That many prophets and righteous *men* have desired to see *those things* which ye see, and have

> not seen *them*; and to hear *those things* which ye hear and have not heard *them*. (Matt.13:17)
>
> **Hear ye therefore the parable of the sower.** (Matt.13:18)

(We will study the parable of the sower in the next chapter — The Tares)

> **All these things spake Jesus unto the multitude in parables; and without a parable spake he not unto them:** (Matt.13:34)
>
> **That it might be fulfilled which was spoken by the prophet, saying, I will open my mouth in parables; I will utter things which have been kept secret from the foundation of the world.** (Matt.13:35).

To understand the true meaning of the phrase "the foundation of the world," we need to know the translation of two Greek words. "Foundation" in the New Testament is *"themelios"* and *"katabole."*

The term *"themelios"* (Strong's Concordance #G2310) is something put down, i.e. a substruction (of a building, etc.), (literally or figuratively) — foundation.

For example, when Jesus said,

"He is like a man which built an house, and digged deep, and laid the foundation on a rock: …" (Lk.6:48)

So, *"themelios"* is the English word translated for "foundation."

The *"katabole"* (Strong's Concordance #G2602): from *kataballo*; a deposition, i.e. founding; figuratively, conception — conceive, foundation.

> *kataballo* (Strong's Concordance #G2598): to throw down — cast down, descend, fall (down), lay.

The word "foundation" of Matthew 13:35 was translated from the Greek word *"katabole:"*

"... I will utter things which have been kept secret from the foundation of the world."

Therefore; the phrase "the foundation of the world," is the casting down or the overthrow of the world. It is the ruin of the previous world; it was the world before the creation of this present world.

To avoid confusion, perhaps it is helpful to know that there was a world before this present world that we're living in now. It's the same earth, but different world ages or two different periods of time. As it is written in the book of Genesis:

"In the beginning God created the heaven and the earth." (Gen.1:1)

The "beginning" is all the way back to the origin, the beginning of time, and that was very long time ago. This was the first earth age, and the founding of the world.

"And, Thou, Lord, in the beginning hast laid the foundation of the earth; and the heavens are the works of thine hands:" (Heb.1:10)

When Satan rebelled against God, some of God's children by their own choice, joined Satan and turned against God also. So with God's fierce anger, God Almighty destroyed that world; God destroyed everything except the souls of His children. This is the reason why the earth became void and without form — it was totally void, and that brought the first earth age to an end. That was the "*katabole*" of the world. Therefore the next verse of the book of Genesis reads:

"And the earth was (*became*) **without form, and void; and darkness was upon the face of the deep."** (Gen.1:2)

It was a beautiful world, because God Almighty did not create the earth without form, but God formed it to be inhabited. It was due to the *katabole*, that the earth (not <u>was</u>, but) <u>became</u> void and without form:

> **For thus saith the LORD that created the heavens; God himself that formed the earth and made it; he hath established it, he created it not in vain, he formed it to be inhabited: I *am* the LORD; and *there is* none else.** (Isa. 45:18)

The overthrow (*katabole*) itself is also written in the book of Jeremiah 4:22–27:

> **For my people *is* foolish, they have not known me; they *are* sottish** (*silly*) **children, and they have none understanding: they *are* wise to do evil, but to do good they have no knowledge.** (Jer.4:22)

I beheld the earth, and, lo, *it was* without form, and void; and the heavens, and they *had* no light. (Jer.4:23)

I beheld the mountains, and, lo, they trembled, and all the hills moved lightly. (Jer.4:24)

I beheld, and, lo, *there was* no man, and all the birds of the heavens were fled. (Jer.4:25)

I beheld, and, lo, the fruitful place *was* a wilderness, and all the cities thereof were broken down at the presence of the LORD, *and* by his fierce anger. (Jer.4:26)

For thus hath the LORD said, The whole land shall be desolate; yet will I not make a full end. (Jer.4:27)

The apostle Peter described the "*katabole*" as;

"… <u>the world that then was</u>, being overflowed with water, perished:" (2Peter 3:6)

Peter was talking about the flood that destroyed the first world age (long before the time of Noah, therefore it is not Noah's flood). Then Peter continued to describe the present world age (the Age of Salvation), and the next world age that is coming. This future world age will last for eternity:

"But <u>the heavens and the earth, which are now</u>, by the same word are kept in store, reserved unto fire against the day of judgment and perdition of ungodly men." (2Peter 3:7)

This time God will no longer use water, but fire to destroy this world age. Please know and understand this; "For our God *is* a consuming fire." (Heb.12:29) It is a cleansing fire, and God's fire will only consume evil in this world, and only the good will remain. It is just like purifying gold with fire, it burns away all the impurities and what remains is only the pure gold. This will be fulfilled at the second coming of the Lord Jesus Christ.

Then after the end of this world age, at the end of the thousand years (Rev.20:5), comes the new heavens and the new earth, the third heaven and earth age:

"Nevertheless we, according to his promise, look for **new heavens and a new earth**, wherein dwelleth righteousness." (2Peter 3:13)

Collected here are the ten verses that the phrase "the foundation of the world" appear in the word of God; seven of them are "from" the foundation of the world, and the other three are "before" the foundation of the world:

> 1. **That it might be fulfilled which was spoken by the prophet, saying, I will open my mouth in parables; I will utter things which have been kept secret from the foundation of the world.** (Matt.13:35)
>
> 2. **Then shall the King say unto them on his right hand, Come, ye blessed of my Father, inherit the kingdom prepared for you from the foundation of the world:** (Matt.25:34)

3. That the blood of all the prophets, which was shed from the foundation of the world, may be required of this generation; (Lk.11:50)

4. For we which have believed do enter into rest, as he said, As I have sworn in my wrath, if they shall enter into my rest: although the works were finished from the foundation of the world. (Heb.4:3)

5. For then must he often have suffered since the foundation of the world: but now once in the end of the world hath he appeared to put away sin by the sacrifice of himself. (Heb.9:26)

6. And all that dwell upon the earth shall worship him, whose names are not written in the book of life of the Lamb slain from the foundation of the world. (Rev.13:8)

7. The beast that thou sawest was, and is not; and shall ascend out of the bottomless pit, and go into perdition: and they that dwell on the earth shall wonder, whose names were not written in the book of life from the foundation of the world, when they behold the beast that was, and is not, and yet is. (Rev.17:8).

1. Father, I will that they also, whom thou hast given me, be with me where I am; that they may behold my glory, which thou hast given me: for thou lovedst me before the foundation of the world. (John 17:24)

> 2. **According as he hath chosen us in him before the foundation of the world, that we should be holy and without blame before him in love:** (Eph.1:4)
>
> 3. **Who verily was foreordained before the foundation of the world, but was manifest in these last times for you,** (1Peter 1:20).

When Jesus Christ started His ministry, which lasted approximately three years (began with His baptism, and ended with His crucifixion), many heard His teachings, many witnessed the miracles He performed, and many of them believed. However, some simply could not comprehend the Word of God, it was difficult for them to accept the teachings of Christ. For example, when Jesus said:

> **This is the bread which cometh down from heaven, that a man may eat thereof, and not die.** (John 6:50)
>
> **I am the living bread which came down from heaven: if any man eat of this bread, he shall live for ever: and the bread that I will give is my flesh, which I will give for the life of the world.** (John 6:51)
>
> **The Jews therefore strove among themselves, saying, How can this man give us *his* flesh to eat?** (John 6:52)

Since they did not understand what Christ was saying, they murmured, they argued among themselves, and they all got upset. But Christ was talking about the Word of God that became "flesh," the Word of God had been born in the flesh, and that is the Lord Jesus Christ, the living Word of God. As it is written:

> In the beginning was the Word, and the Word was with God, and the Word was God. (John 1:1)

> And the Word was made flesh, and dwelt among us, (and we beheld his glory, the glory as of the only begotten of the Father,) full of grace and truth. (John 1:14)

The prophecy of the Messiah had been fulfilled:

"… Behold, a virgin shall conceive, and bear a son, and shall call his name Immanuel." (Isa.7:14)

God in the flesh, Christ is the living bread which is the spiritual bread, standing in front of them and was talking to them; "and his name is called The Word of God." (Rev.19:13)

> Then Jesus said unto them, Verily, verily, I say unto you, Except ye eat the flesh of the Son of man, and drink his blood, ye have no life in you. (John 6:53)

> Whoso eateth my flesh, and drinketh my blood, hath eternal life; and I will raise him up at the last day. (John 6:54)

Jesus was letting them know that unless they eat (learn and understand) the Word of God, and drink His blood for the remission of sins, accepting Him as Lord and Savior, then they have no eternal life, because:

"It is the spirit that quickeneth (*give life*); the flesh profiteth nothing: the words that I speak unto you, *they* are spirit, and *they* are life." (John 6:63)

Therefore to hear the word of God with understanding is very important, it is the only way to gain the knowledge of the truth, and it is the only way to have life and live eternally. Jesus told Satan the same thing, when He quoted Deuteronomy chapter 8 verse 3:

"**It is written, Man shall not live by bread alone, but by every word that proceedeth out of the mouth of God.**" (Matt.4:4)

Hearing God's word with understanding will guide people to do things the right way, God's way, and give whosoever would believe in Jesus Christ the opportunity to:

> **Being born again, not of corruptible seed, but of incorruptible, by the word of God, which liveth and abideth for ever.** (1Peter 1:23)
>
> **Even when we were dead in sins, hath quickened us together with Christ, (by grace ye are saved;)** (Eph.2:5).

By the grace of God, we are made alive in Christ, that is "spiritually alive." That is why blessed are those have eyes to see and ears to hear.

The two rich men recorded in the book of Luke are good examples; One man went by the name of Zacchaeus. He was a short man, who was a chief tax collector, and was desperately seeking to know more about Jesus.

According to the Bible 23

After meeting with Jesus, Zacchaeus realized that he was spiritually dead and needed the Savior. He knew some of the things he did were wrong (e.g. over-taxing people, making unfair deals, etc.). Zacchaeus believed in the Lord Jesus Christ and he sincerely repented. So he voluntarily proposed to give half of his possessions to the poor and to pay back four times the amount to anyone he defrauded (Lk.19:2–10). However, the other rich man was unwilling to do the same, and it was very difficult for him to unload his ill-gotten gains (Lk.18:18–23).

> **And, behold, *there was* a man named Zacchaeus, which was the chief among the publicans, and he was rich.** (Lk.19:2)
>
> **And he sought to see Jesus who he was; and could not for the press, because he was little of stature.** (Lk.19:3)
>
> **And he ran before, and climbed up into a sycomore tree to see him: for he was to pass that *way*.** (Lk.19:4)
>
> **And when Jesus came to the place, he looked up, and saw him, and said unto him, Zacchaeus, make haste, and come down; for to-day I must abide at thy house.** (Lk.19:5)
>
> **And he made haste, and came down, and received him joyfully.** (Lk.19:6)
>
> **And when they saw *it*, they all murmured, saying, That he was gone to be guest with a man that is a sinner.** (Lk.19:7)
>
> **And Zacchaeus stood, and said unto the Lord; Behold, Lord, the half of my goods I give to the poor; and if I have taken

> any thing from any man by false accusation, I restore *him* fourfold. (Lk.19:8)
>
> And Jesus said unto him, This day is salvation come to this house, forsomuch as he also is a son of Abraham. (Lk.19:9)
>
> For the Son of man is come to seek and to save that which was lost. (Lk.19:10)

There is nothing wrong with being rich, if it was gained through hard work and in an honest way, God's way. It is not a sin for being wealthy, it is delightful to Almighty God, if people accumulate wealth or gain riches through an honest way. However, it is an abomination to the LORD for anyone to gain wealth through dishonest or taking advantage of others:

> Shall I count *them* pure with the wicked balances, and with the bag of deceitful weights? (Micah 6:11)
>
> A FALSE balance *is* abomination to the LORD: but a just weight *is* his delight. (Prov.11:1)

So it is important to bear in mind and understand that we are talking about ill-gotten riches, wealth from dishonest gain.

> And a certain ruler asked him, saying, Good Master, what shall I do to inherit eternal life? (Lk.18:18)
>
> And Jesus said unto him, Why callest thou me good? none *is* good, save (*but*) one, *that is*, God. (Lk.18:19)

> Thou knowest the commandments, Do not commit adultery, Do not kill, Do not steal, Do not bear false witness, Honour thy father and thy mother. (Lk.18:20)
>
> And he said, All these have I kept from my youth up. (Lk.18:21)
>
> Now when Jesus heard these things, he said unto him, Yet lackest thou one thing: sell all that thou hast, and distribute unto the poor, and thou shalt have treasure in heaven: and come, follow me. (Lk.18:22)
>
> And when he heard this, he was very sorrowful: for he was very rich. (Lk.18:23)

Jesus knew what was in the heart of the rich man, and said, "Yet lackest thou one thing:" What Jesus is saying to the rich man was that he got a lot of ill-gotten gains that he had to get rid of them. That's why Jesus left out one of the civil laws from the ten commandments, (which belong to our relationship with people) because the rich man had broken it, that is, not to covet anything that belongs to a fellow-countryman:

> Thou shalt not covet thy neighbour's house, thou shalt not covet thy neighbour's wife, nor his manservant, nor his maidservant, nor his ox, nor his ass, nor any thing that *is* thy neighbour's. (Ex.20:17)

God knows everything about us, nothing is hidden to Almighty God. He can read our heart or mind. Jesus knows what was in their hearts. As it is written:

> **Shall not God search this out? for he knoweth the secrets of the heart.** (Psalm 44:21).
>
> **… for the LORD searcheth all hearts, and understandeth all the imaginations of the thoughts: if thou seek him, he will be found of thee; but if thou forsake him, he will cast thee off for ever.** (1Chron.28:9).

Therefore Jesus' answer to the latter rich man's question, was a bitter pill for him to swallow. For those that still want to keep their ill-gotten wealth, unfortunately, will be prevented from entering the kingdom of God. Because no man can serve Almighty God while chasing wealth and riches through dishonest ways with evil in their hearts.

> **And when Jesus saw that he was very sorrowful, he said, How hardly shall they that have riches enter into the kingdom of God!** (Lk.18:24)
>
> **For it is easier for a camel to go through a needle's eye, than for a rich man to enter into the kingdom of God.** (Lk.18:25)

When night fell, access from the main gate to the city was closed, and a small door called the "needle gate" was used for security reasons. So for a camel to pass through the needle gate, they must be unloaded of luggage. For this reason, symbolically it was the difficulty of the latter rich man — to unload his ill-gotten riches.

> **"And they that heard *it* said, Who then can be saved?"** (Lk.18:26)

The answer to that question is obviously no one. This is because we must obey all the ten commandments, and if we break just one of them, we basically break them all. And for anyone, rich or poor alike, male or female, young and old, that is just an impossibility to go through life in this world age without breaking one of God's commandments. No one is good enough to be able to keep them all. That is why back in Luke 18:19, Jesus said no one is good, except God alone. It is written:

> **For whosoever shall keep the whole law, and yet offend in one *point*, he is guilty of all.** (James 2:10)
>
> **All we like sheep have gone astray; we have turned every one to his own way; and the LORD hath laid on him the iniquity of us all.** (Isa.53:6)

The Ten Commandments is a perfect set of laws, but clearly it can save no one. This is simply because, it is impossible for anyone to keep them all. No one can save himself by observing these laws nor can anyone save another. That is why God our Heavenly Father sent His only begotten Son, the Lord Jesus the Christ, the Savior of the world for us.

> **For God sent not his Son into the world to condemn the world; but that the world through him might be saved.** (John 3:17)
>
> **I am the way, the truth, and the life: no man cometh unto the Father, but by me.** (John 14:6)

The only way to God's kingdom is God's Way, the only truth is God's Word, and the only way to eternal life is by following the Lord and Savior Jesus the Christ.

"And he said, The things which are impossible with men are possible with God." (Lk.18:27)

Without help from God, there are many things that are impossible with men. There is no way for anyone that can acquire everlasting life by their own effort. Again, it is because we must obey all of God's laws, and we already know that it is an impossibility. Fortunately, the Heavenly Father provided us the Way, the only possible way, that we may be able to inherit that everlasting life, and that is through the Savior of the world. Everything is possible with Jesus the Christ (Emmanuel — "God with us"):

"In whom we have redemption through his blood, *even* the forgiveness of sins:" (Col.1:14)

The death and the resurrection of Jesus Christ made it possible. Our sins today are covered by the precious blood of Jesus Christ. He died on the cross for the sins of the world, that on breaking the commandments of God, whosoever that would believe upon Him can sincerely repent and ask God for forgiveness, on sincere repentance it is forgiven. So, indeed it is possible with God.

However there was a small group of people, not only did they refuse to believe, they were also very determined to kill Jesus Christ. They wanted to eliminate the Savior of the world. But why

According to the Bible 29

and who were these people that are so determined to kill the Christ? John the Baptist called them the "generation of vipers" (offspring of serpents) in the book of Matthew.

The word "generation" was translated from the Greek word *gennema* (Strong's Concordance #G1081), and its definition is: offspring; by analogy, produce (literally or figuratively): — fruit, generation:

> **"But when he saw many of the Pharisees and Sadducees come to his baptism, he said unto them, O generation of vipers, who hath warned you to flee from the wrath to come?"** (Matt.3:7)

Jesus Christ also called them the "generation of vipers" in the following verses:

> **O generation of vipers, how can ye, being evil, speak good things? for out of the abundance of the heart the mouth speaketh.** (Matt.12:34)
>
> **Ye serpents, *ye* generation of vipers, how can ye escape the damnation of hell?** (Matt.23:33)

This is an important statement from both John the Baptist and from the Lord Jesus Christ, naming the "generation of vipers." Why would they call these group of people the children of serpents? That is because of the old serpent in the Garden of Eden, he is Satan the devil, written in the book of Genesis chapter three.

The book of Revelation makes it very clear who the serpent is:

> **And the great dragon was cast out, that old serpent, called the Devil, and Satan, which deceiveth the whole world: he**

was cast out into the earth, and his angels were cast out with him. (Rev.12:9)

Jesus made it very clear and easy to understand while He was speaking to the same group of people when He said:

Ye are of *your* father the devil, and the lusts of your father ye will do. He was a murderer from the beginning, and abode not in the truth, because there is no truth in him. When he speaketh a lie, he speaketh of his own: for he is a liar, and the father of it. (John 8:44)

Falsehood puts people in bondage (spiritually speaking), but knowing and understanding the word of God, which is the truth, will set people free:

Then said Jesus to those Jews which believed on him, If ye continue in my word, *then* are ye my disciples indeed; (John 8:31)

And ye shall know the truth, and the truth shall make you free. (John 8:32)

The truth will set people free from anxiety, the truth will set people free from all confusion in God's word, and the truth will set people free from the misunderstanding between the children of the kingdom and the children of the wicked one, that is the old serpent the devil.

According to the Bible

As we can see that there are two distinct fathers in this present world age. Firstly, our heavenly Father (upper cased) the Creator of all things, our Maker:

> **Hast thou not known? hast thou not heard, *that* the everlasting God, the LORD, the Creator of the ends of the earth, fainteth not, neither is weary?** *there is* **no searching of his understanding.** (Isa.40:28)
>
> **O come, let us worship and bow down: let us kneel before the LORD our maker.** (Psalm 95:6)

Secondly, the other father — their father (lower cased) the devil, the destroyer, the trouble maker:

> **Ye are of *your* father the devil, and the lusts of your father ye will do.** (John 8:44)
>
> **And they had a king over them, *which is* the angel of the bottomless pit, whose name in the Hebrew tongue *is* Abaddon, but in the Greek tongue hath *his* name Apollyon.** (Rev.9:11)

Abaddon (Strong's Concordance #G3): a destroying angel.

Apollyon (Strong's Concordance #G623): a destroyer (i.e. Satan).

Through the death of Jesus Christ in the flesh and blood, Christ destroyed the destroyer. Christ destroyed (to become of no effect; powerless) "death," that is, Satan the devil. Christ destroyed their father the devil that had the power of death. Because through lies and deception, he causes people to sin against God and die spiritually, that is the "spiritual death."

> **Forasmuch then as the children are partakers of flesh and blood, he also himself likewise took part of the same; that through death he might destroy him that had the power of death, that is, the devil;** (Heb.2:14)
>
> **For the wages of sin *is* death; but the gift of God *is* eternal life through Jesus Christ our Lord.** (Rom.6:23)

There are also two different Christ's — The Messiah, Jesus the Christ, and the Antichrist, the false Christ (the "instead-of-Christ").

The word "antichrist" was translated from the Greek word "*antichristos*" (Strong's Concordance #G500) which comes from two Greek words — *anti* and *christos*; an opponent of the Messiah.

The Greek word "*anti*" (Strong's Concordance #G473) means opposite, i.e. instead or because of (rarely in addition to) — substitution.

The Greek word "*christos*" (Strong's Concordance #G5547) means anointed, i.e. the Messiah, an epithet of Jesus — Christ.

So, the Antichrist is the "instead-of-Christ," in other words, instead of the real Christ, it is the fake Christ.

According to the Bible

One-time Jesus was asked by His disciples privately about His second coming. Before Christ gave all the details concerning His second coming, first He gave them a warning to beware of antichrist before His return. Instead of Him (the true Christ) the Antichrist will appear, standing in the holy place and claiming to be the Messiah. Certainly, many will be deceived, many will worship him, not knowing he is the false Christ:

> **And as he sat upon the mount of Olives, the disciples came unto him privately, saying, Tell us, when shall these things be? and what *shall be* the sign of thy coming, and of the end of the world?** (Matt.24:3)
>
> **And Jesus answered and said unto them, Take heed that no man deceive you.** (Matt.24:4)
>
> **For many shall come in my name, saying, I am Christ; and shall deceive many.** (Matt.24:5)
>
> **When ye therefore shall see the abomination of desolation,** (*desolator* — *the Antichrist*) **spoken of by Daniel the prophet,** (*Dan.9:27*) **stand in the holy place, (whoso readeth, let him understand:)** (Matt.24:15)
>
> **Then if any man shall say unto you, Lo, here *is* Christ, or there; believe *it* not.** (Matt.24:23)

Apostle Paul gave the same warning for the appearance of the Antichrist: Do not let anyone mislead you into this belief that Jesus Christ has already returned, do not believe it. Paul emphasized two things must happen first before the return of the true Messiah, the real Jesus Christ. First is the "falling away" (apostasy), and then second, the revealing of the "son of perdition" which is none other than Satan the devil, claiming to be the Messiah in the temple of God, claiming that he is the Christ!

> **Now we beseech you, brethren, by the coming of our Lord Jesus Christ, and *by* our gathering together unto him,** (2Thess.2:1)
>
> **That ye be not soon shaken in mind, or be troubled, neither by spirit, nor by word, nor by letter as from us, as that the day of Christ is at hand.** (2Thess.2:2)
>
> **Let no man deceive you by any means: for *that day shall not come*, except there come a falling away first, and that man of sin be revealed, the son of perdition;** (2Thess.2:3)
>
> **Who opposeth and exalteth himself above all that is called God, or that is worshipped; so that he as God sitteth in the temple of God, shewing himself that he is God.** (2Thess.2:4)

Gaining the knowledge of the truth provided in this book will leave no room for deception by the Antichrist, that is the false Christ, the son of perdition, the destroyer of the soul.

Chapter 2

The Tares

One mystery or hidden truth discussed in this book takes place in the Garden of Eden. It involves Adam, Eve, the serpent and their children. The Parable of the Tares of the Field was taught by the Lord Jesus Christ and explained to His disciples in detail. Although there were detailed explanations, it may be difficult to fully understand, or simply to accept them. For some people it may even cause more confusion. This is exactly the way the devil wants it, for the people to be confused about the truth, and to be confused about the Word of God. It is Satan the devil that wants to hide the truth, and one is the truth about what he did in the Garden of Eden. It was that old serpent the devil who planted the tares of the field. As Jesus Christ said in the book of Matthew:

> **… the tares are the children of the wicked *one*;** (Matt.13:38)
>
> **The enemy that sowed them is the devil; …** (Matt.13:39)
>
> **Every plant, which my heavenly Father hath not planted, shall be rooted up.** (Matt.15:13)

To understand the Parable of the Tares of the Field, we need to learn from both the old testament and the new testament. We cannot fully understand the new testament without knowing the old testament, and of course vice versa.

In the new testament Jesus Christ talks about the children of the devil in a parable, which describe what Satan the devil did in the beginning at the Garden of Eden. With knowledge and understanding of the Old Testament, it is easier to comprehend the Parable of the Tares of the Field.

First, let us start solving the "Parable of the Sower." Although it is very similar to the "Parable of the Tares," they are about two totally different subjects. We need to know two Greek terms in which the English word "seed" was translated from (*speiro* or *sperma*), because both parables used the word "seed" as a symbol of something that was sown.

The Greek word "*speiro*" (Strong's Concordance #G4687) means to scatter, i.e. sow (literally or figuratively); — sow (–er), receive seed.

The seed (*speiro*) in the Parable of the Sower represents the word of God, and this type of sowing is scattering seeds. Therefore, it is the scattering of the word of God, an example of this is by way of broadcasting the word of God in public, through radio, television, internet by the teachers of God's word:

> **And he spake many things unto them in parables, saying, Behold, a sower went forth to sow;** (Matt.13:3)
>
> **And when he sowed, some *seeds* fell by the way side, and the fowls came and devoured them up:** (Matt.13:4)

> Some fell upon stony places, where they had not much earth: and forthwith they sprung up, because they had no deepness of earth: (Matt.13:5)
>
> And when the sun was up, they were scorched; and because they had no root, they withered away. (Matt.13:6)
>
> And some fell among thorns; and the thorns sprung up, and choked them: (Matt.13:7)
>
> But other fell into good ground, and brought forth fruit, some an hundredfold, some sixtyfold, some thirtyfold. (Matt.13:8)
>
> Who hath ears to hear, let him hear. (Matt.13:9)

Then Jesus explained the parable of the sower. It is important to note that there is a big difference between hearing the word of God and hearing the word of God with *understanding*.

> Hear ye therefore the parable of the sower. (Matt.13:18)
>
> When any one heareth the word of the kingdom, and understandeth *it* not, then cometh the wicked *one*, and catcheth away that which was sown in his heart. This is he which received seed by the way side. (Matt.13:19)
>
> But he that received the seed into stony places, the same is he that heareth the word, and anon with joy receiveth it; (Matt.13:20)
>
> Yet hath he not root in himself, but dureth for a while: for when tribulation or persecution ariseth because of the word, by and by he is offended. (Matt.13:21)

> He also that received seed among the thorns is he that heareth the word; and the care of this world, and the deceitfulness of riches, choke the word, and he becometh unfruitful. (Matt.13:22)
>
> But he that received seed into the good ground is he that heareth the word, and understandeth *it*; which also beareth fruit, and bringeth forth, some an hundredfold, some sixty, some thirty. (Matt.13:23)

Now, the "seed" in the Parable of the Tares of the Field no longer represents the word of God, but it represents people, because the "seed" was translated from the Greek word "*sperma*."

The Greek word "*sperma*" (Strong's Concordance #G4690) means something sown, i.e. seed (including the male "*sperm*"); by implication, offspring; specially, a remnant (figuratively, as if kept over for planting).

> Another parable put he forth unto them, saying, The kingdom of heaven is likened unto a man which sowed good seed in his field: (Matt.13:24)
>
> But while men slept, his enemy came and sowed tares among the wheat, and went his way. (Matt.13:25)
>
> But when the blade was sprung up, and brought forth fruit, then appeared the tares also. (Matt.13:26)

> So the servants of the householder came and said unto him, Sir, didst not thou sow good seed in thy field? from whence then hath it tares? (Matt.13:27)
>
> He said unto them, An enemy hath done this. The servants said unto him, Wilt thou then that we go and gather them up? (Matt.13:28)
>
> But he said, Nay; lest while ye gather up the tares, ye root up also the wheat with them. (Matt.13:29)
>
> Let both grow together until the harvest: and in the time of harvest I will say to the reapers, Gather ye together first the tares, and bind them in bundles to burn them: but gather the wheat into my barn. (Matt.13:30)

The disciples asked Jesus privately to explain to them the parable of the tares of the field, because they still did not understand it totally. Therefore, these explanations are now facts — not something that is symbolism, not an allegory, not a figure of speech or metaphor. As we can see this is a private teaching to His disciples, and the mystery in the Garden of Eden is about to be revealed:

> Then Jesus sent the multitude away, and went into the house: and his disciples came unto him, saying, Declare unto us the parable of the tares of the field. (Matt.13:36)
>
> He answered and said unto them, He that soweth the good seed is the Son of man; (Matt.13:37)

In other words, the man who "sowed the good seed" is the Almighty God the Creator of all things, as it is written in the book of Genesis:

> **And God said, Let us make man** (*mankind*) **in our image, after our likeness:** ... (Gen.1:26)
>
> ... **male and female created he them.** (Gen.1:27)

Then brought forth Adam and Eve:

> **And the LORD God formed man** *of* **the dust of the ground, and breathed into his nostrils the breath of life; and man became a living soul.** (Gen.2:7)
>
> **And the LORD God caused a deep sleep to fall upon Adam, and he slept: and he took one of his ribs, and closed up the flesh instead thereof**; (Gen.2:21)
>
> **And the rib, which the LORD God had taken from man, made he a woman, and brought her unto the man.** (Gen.2:22).
>
> **And Adam called his wife's name Eve; because she was the mother of all living.** (Gen.3:20).

However, after God Almighty created all the children on the "field," which is this present world age that we live in, the devil then, through deception, managed to produce his own children which are the "tares."

> **The field is the world; the good seed are the children of the kingdom; but the tares are the children of the wicked** *one*; (Matt.13:38)

> The enemy that sowed them is the devil; the harvest is the end of the world; and the reapers are the angels. (Matt.13:39)

The "wicked one" and "the enemy" is Satan of course, and he sowed the tares (more detail in chapter 3 — "Don't Eat, Don't Touch"). The "harvest" is the end of this world age, and that is when the true Christ returns. The "reapers" are the angels who will deal with the "tares," so this is why God told the servants to leave the tares alone and do not get involved with them.

> As therefore the tares are gathered and burned in the fire; so shall it be in the end of this world. (Matt.13:40)

> The Son of man shall send forth his angels, and they shall gather out of his kingdom all things that offend, and them which do iniquity; (Matt.13:41)

> And shall cast them into a furnace of fire: there shall be wailing and gnashing of teeth. (Matt.13:42)

> Then shall the righteous shine forth as the sun in the kingdom of their Father. Who hath ears to hear, let him hear. (Matt.13:43)

The "tares" were living among the regular people who were unaware of it. They could not tell or recognize the "tares," because they look just like normal people. It is hard to know and to differentiate the children of the devil and the children of God.

Similarly, in the Parable of the Tares of the Field, the tares look just like wheat, so it is difficult to differentiate the tares and the wheat. However, when they produced fruit, the servants could then differentiate between the tares and the wheat. As Jesus said: "Ye shall know them by their fruits." (Matt.7:16)

The "tares" were claiming to be descendants of Abraham, saying, "We be Abraham's seed." However, at the same time (as they may not realize it), they were also saying that they are not Abraham's descendants when they said, "and were never in bondage to any man."

> **They answered him, We be Abraham's seed, and were never in bondage to any man: how sayest thou, Ye shall be made free?** (John 8:33)

Perhaps they are simply confused of the origin of their pedigree, because Abraham's seed was in bondage for four hundred years!

> **And he said unto Abram, Know of a surety that thy seed shall be a stranger in a land *that is* not theirs, and shall serve them; and they shall afflict them four hundred years;** (Gen.15:13)

> **And God spake on this wise, That his seed should sojourn in a strange land; and that they should bring them into bondage, and entreat *them* evil four hundred years.** (Acts 7:6)

So indeed, they are not Abraham's seed, nor are they who think or claim to be; as Jesus Christ called them, the "tares," sowed by their father the devil.

> **Jesus saith unto them, If ye were Abraham's children, ye would do the works of Abraham.** (John 8:39)
>
> **But now ye seek to kill me, a man that hath told you the truth, which I have heard of God:** (John 8:40)
>
> **Ye are of *your* father the devil, and the lusts of your father ye will do.** (John 8:44)

While Jesus was busy teaching, healing, and performing mighty miracles, they (the tares) were also busy taking counsel, conspiring on how they can kill the Christ.

Satan himself had been trying to do the same since the foundation of the world. He tried to prevent the first prophecy of the Bible from coming to pass (Gen.3:15). Because the LORD God declared that the Seed (Christ) of the woman will bruise his (Satan's) head. If Satan succeeded in preventing the birth of the Christ, the Word of God would have failed, and then his own death sentence (Ezk.28:18–19) would be avoided:

> **And I will put enmity between thee and the woman, and between thy seed and her seed; it shall bruise thy head, and thou shalt bruise his heel."** (Gen.3:15)

Therefore, Satan tried to corrupt the woman's seed line through which Christ would be born from, to prevent the perfect birth of Jesus Christ from the daughters of Adam. Because Jesus the Christ is the only one that can and will execute Satan's death sentence, and it was fulfilled and accomplished on the cross:

> Thou hast defiled thy sanctuaries by the multitude of thine iniquities, by the iniquity of thy traffick; therefore will I bring forth a fire from the midst of thee, it shall devour thee, and I will bring thee to ashes upon the earth in the sight of all them that behold thee. (Ezk.28:18)
>
> All they that know thee among the people shall be astonished at thee: thou shalt be a terror, and never *shalt* thou *be* any more. (Ezk.28:19)

Satan's purpose of corrupting the woman's seed line was an irruption of fallen angels (sons of God), recorded in the book of Genesis (Gen.6:1–7). They married the daughters of men, and had children born to them — the giants (*Nephilim*), and they had to be destroyed. This is the reason for the flood. Only Noah and his family preserved their pedigree and kept it perfectly pure from Adam, all the rest had become corrupt:

> And the LORD said, I will destroy man whom I have created from the face of the earth; both man, and beast, and the creeping thing, and the fowls of the air; for it repenteth me that I have made them. (Gen.6:7)
>
> But Noah found grace in the eyes of the LORD. (Gen.6:8)
>
> ... Noah was a just man *and* perfect in his generations, *and* Noah walked with God. (Gen.6:9)

As soon as it was made known that Christ would be born from Abram and his wife Sarai, Satan continued trying to interfere with the seed line. So God had to intervene. "And the LORD plagued Pharaoh and his house with great plagues because of Sarai Abram's wife." (Gen.12:17) Divine intervention from the LORD was necessary to protect the perfect birth of Jesus Christ:

> **Now the LORD had said unto Abram, Get thee out of thy country, and from thy kindred, and from thy father's house, unto a land that I will shew thee:** (Gen.12:1)
>
> **And I will make of thee a great nation, and I will bless thee, and make thy name great; and thou shalt be a blessing:** (Gen.12:2)
>
> **And I will bless them that bless thee, and curse him that curseth thee: and in thee shall all families of the earth be blessed.** (Gen.12:3)

Note the phrase "and in thee" — again through Abraham would come the promised "Seed," that is the Lord Jesus Christ. If we're in Christ then we are blessed indeed; "shall all families of the earth be blessed" — Gentiles included, such that whomsoever believes in Jesus Christ the Savior of the world is blessed.

As the apostle Paul said, God announced the Gospel (God's salvation through Christ) in advance to Abraham. (Of course, it was not good news for Satan, because he knew it would be the end of him! This was the sole motive he had when desperately interfering the immaculate birth of Jesus the Christ):

> **And the scripture, foreseeing that God would justify the heathen through faith, preached before the gospel unto**

> Abraham, *saying*, In thee shall all nations be blessed. (Gal.3:8)
>
> That the blessing of Abraham might come on the Gentiles through Jesus Christ; that we might receive the promise of the Spirit through faith. (Gal.3:14)
>
> And if ye *be* Christ's, then are ye Abraham's seed, and heirs according to the promise. (Gal.3:29)

Through the gospel, Gentiles who believe in the Lord Jesus Christ become "spiritual seed" of Abraham, hence heirs according to the promise.

> That the Gentiles should be fellow-heirs, and of the same body and partakers of his promise in Christ by the gospel: (Eph.3:6).

Abraham was a father of many nations or a blessing to many nations — that is the reason why Almighty God changed Abram's (*a high father*) name to Abraham (*father of a multitude*):

> Neither shall thy name any more be called Abram, but thy name shall be Abraham; for a father of many nations have I made thee. (Gen.17:5)

Satan attempted many times to interfere and destroy the seed of the woman (Gen.3:15). It can be seen throughout the Bible, where divine intervention occurred each time, to protect the perfect birth of Jesus the Christ — God's plan of Salvation for us. The word of the Lord spoken by the prophet Isaiah (Isa.7:14) was then fulfilled:

> Now all this was done, that it might be fulfilled which was spoken of the Lord by the prophet, saying, (Matt.1:22)
>
> Behold, a virgin shall be with child, and shall bring forth a son, and they shall call his name Emmanuel, which being interpreted is, God with us. (Matt.1:23)

One of the first attempts by Satan to kill the Christ was after baby Jesus was born. Satan did this through Herod the king, who commanded all male children under two years old in Bethlehem to be slain (Matt.2:16). Divine Intervention was needed, thus:

> ... behold, the angel of the Lord appeareth to Joseph in a dream, saying, Arise, and take the young child and his mother, and flee into Egypt, and be thou there until I bring thee word: for Herod will seek the young child to destroy him. (Matt.2:13)
>
> When he arose, he took the young child and his mother by night, and departed into Egypt: (Matt.2:14)
>
> And was there until the death of Herod: that it might be fulfilled which was spoken of the Lord by the prophet, (Hosea 11:1) saying, Out of Egypt have I called my son. (Matt.2:15)

Persistent, Satan next attempt was after Jesus' baptism by the prophet John the Baptist. Satan himself tried to kill Christ by deliberately misquoting scriptures, by adding and omitting words. Satan suggested that Jesus can throw Himself down from the top of the highest point of the Temple, because He will be supported and protected from harm by angels "at any time." Satan said to Jesus:

> **... If thou be the Son of God, cast thyself down: for it is written, He shall give his angels charge concerning thee: and in *their* hands they shall bear thee up, lest at any time thou dash thy foot against a stone.** (Matt.4:6)

But that's not what the scripture says! Scripture did not say "at any time," but what was written is "to keep thee in all thy ways" — that is God's way, God's manner of doing things, God's law. What Satan said to Jesus was in fact contrary to the word of God.

Let us see how Satan distorted God's word. He quoted scriptures from the book of Psalms chapter 91 verses 11 and 12. He omitted the words "to keep thee in all thy ways" from verse 11 and added the words "at any time" into verse 12.

Psalms 91:11-12	Matthew 4:6
	6. And saith unto him, If thou be the Son of God, cast thyself down: for it is written,
11. For he shall give his angels charge over thee, <u>to keep thee in all thy ways.</u>	He shall give his angels charge concerning thee:
12. They shall bear thee up in their hands, lest thou dash thy foot against a stone.	and in *their* hands they shall bear thee up, lest <u>at any time</u> thou dash thy foot against a stone.

Corrupting and twisting God's word was — and still is — one of Satan's greatest method for deceiving souls. Satan used this method of deception on Eve in the Garden of Eden. Likewise, we can see the same strategy Satan tried on Christ, twisting the truth of God's word. Of course, Christ did not fall into Satan's trap.

It was yet another failed attempt of Satan to kill the Christ. Despite of all the failed attempts, Satan will never give up, and he will keep trying. Next, it will be through the "tares," especially through those that are influential and have already established themselves in the house of God as religious leaders and as scribes. They already have taken their place on "Moses' seat." (Moses was the law giver; God gave law to His children through Moses).

In other words, the Scribes and the Pharisees had religious authority and influence (the seat of Moses). They interpreted the law and tried to give law, however it was not lawful, because it was contrary to the word of God. Further, they aside what God commanded, with the purpose of maintaining their own tradition. As Jesus said unto them:

> **Full well ye reject the commandment of God, that ye may keep your own tradition.** (Mk.7:9)
>
> **Making the word of God of none effect through your tradition, which ye have delivered: and many such like things do ye.** (Mk.7:13)

Then Jesus said to the crowd and His disciples, to do whatever the Scribes and the Pharisees told them to do, but not to do as they do, because they don't practice what they preach.

> **Saying, The scribes and the Pharisees sit in Moses' seat:** (Matt.23:2)
>
> **All therefore whatsoever they bid you observe, *that* observe and do; but do not ye after their works: for they say, and do not.** (Matt.23:3)

Again, Jesus Christ Himself called this small group of people, the offspring of snake, that old serpent of the Garden of Eden, the devil:

> ***Ye* serpents, *ye* generation of vipers, how can ye escape the damnation of hell?** (Matt.23:33)

Did not Moses give you the law, and *yet* none of you keepeth the law? Why go ye about to kill me? (John 7:19)

That was not a religiously righteous thing to do; it was totally against Moses' law. ("Thou shalt not kill" — Ex.20:13). But they will follow the strong desires of their father the devil. The Scribes and Pharisees were resourceful, persistent and had murder in their hearts. It was through conspiracy they managed and persuaded others to kill Jesus the Christ by crucifixion.

The word of God never fails. God already foretold this in the book of Genesis: when the LORD said, "and thou (Satan) shalt bruise his (Christ's) heel" (Gen.3:15). Therefore, it must come to pass, and it was being fulfilled when the "tares" manage to deliver Christ to be crucified and nailed Christ's heel on the cross.

Jesus even told the "tares" of their origin and told them what they will do, which is their father's strongest desire — that is, to eliminate the Messiah, to destroy and kill the Christ. So once again, let us listen and learn from the word of God, Jesus' own words.

> **Ye are of *your* father the devil, and the lusts of your father ye will do. He was a murderer** (*a manslayer*) **from the beginning, and abode not in the truth, because there is no truth in him. When he speaketh a lie, he speaketh of his own: for he is a liar, and the father of it.** (John 8:44).

Therefore, Satan was a manslayer from the very beginning, all the way back from the first earth age. Because "death" came through him, he caused death of the angels who followed him before the foundation of the world. Specifically, seven thousand fallen angels have already been sentenced to die; they are the only souls that have already been sentenced to the final death (Rev.11:13).

Then in this present earth age, Satan again will cause many to die spiritually. That is why Almighty God sent His only begotten Son, to the earth, in the flesh, so "that through death he might destroy him that had the power of death, that is, the devil" (Heb.2:14). People need to be spiritually born again to have everlasting life through Jesus the Christ, the Savior of the world. In the Garden of Eden, Satan tempted Eve to sin against God, and Adam also partook of it which brought spiritual death upon them:

"For the wages of sin *is* death; but the gift of God *is* eternal life through Jesus Christ our Lord." (Rom.6:23)

Satan does not want any soul to qualify for the gift of everlasting life through Christ. He does not want any soul to know the truth, thus by distorting God's word, through lies and deception, he causes many to sin: That is Satan's own nature — a liar — "for he is a liar, and the father of it."

The first spoken word and temptation of Satan (to the woman in the Garden of Eden) began with a question — casting doubt on God's word. Because one can be easily deceived when in doubt and confused. Satan said unto the woman:

> Yea, hath God said, Ye shall not eat of every tree of the garden?" (Gen.3:1)
>
> And the woman said unto the serpent, We may eat of the fruit of the trees of the garden: (Gen.3:2)
>
> But of the fruit of the tree which *is* in the midst of the garden, God hath said, Ye shall not eat of it, neither shall ye touch it, lest ye die. (Gen.3:3)

Then here comes the lie of Satan to the woman:

> And the serpent said unto the woman, Ye shall <u>not</u> surely die: (Gen.3:4)

Like father, like son — Cain also lied and even questioned God; he knew exactly where his brother Abel was, because that was just after he murdered Abel.

> And Cain talked with Abel his brother: and it came to pass, when they were in the field, that Cain rose up against Abel his brother, and slew him. (Gen.4:8)
>
> And the LORD said unto Cain, Where *is* Abel thy brother? And he said, I know not: *Am* I my brother's keeper? (Gen.4:9).

According to the word of God, the serpent in the Garden of Eden — Satan the devil was Cain's father. The teaching of Jesus (the Parable of the Tares of the Field) makes it clear that the "tares" were the descendants of Cain called the "Kenites." (We will study and learn more about the "Kenites" in the next chapter — "Don't Eat, Don't Touch").

The word "Kenites" was transliterated from the Hebrew tongue "*Qeyniy*," and it simply means, "the sons of Cain;"

> Strong's Concordance #H7017; *Qeyniy* (*kay-nee'*); Patronymic from 7014; a kenite.
>
> Strong's Concordance #H7014; *Qayin* (*kah'-yin*); Cain.

Therefore, the kenites (the tares) were not Abraham's descendants; they were not Adamic people ... they were the sons of Cain. As it is written in the book of 1Chronicles chapter 2 verse 55, the Rechabites were the Kenites, and they were already "scribes" since then.

> **And the families of the scribes which dwelt at Jabez; the Tirathites, the Shimeathites,** *and* **Suchathites. These** *are* **the Kenites that came of Hemath, the father of the house of Rechab.** (1Chron.2:55)

Also, in the book of Jeremiah chapter 35 verse 11, the Rechabites (Kenites) fled into the walled city of Jerusalem for protection. That is the reason why they were inside Jerusalem, and by residence, that is how they can <u>claim</u> to be of Judah, but they are actually the sons of Cain.

> **But it came to pass, when Nebuchadrezzar king of Babylon came up into the land, that we said, Come, and let us go to Jerusalem for fear of the army of the Chaldeans, and for fear**

of the army of the Syrians: so we dwell at Jerusalem. (Jer.35:11)

The genealogy of Cain is one of the "mysteries" in God's word. However, with the "Key of David" we will be able to unlock the true genealogy of Cain. The key that will unlock the so-called "mystery" is the teaching of Jesus Christ — it is the key that opens one's spiritual eyes that no one else can shut, as truth always prevails. In the book of Revelation Jesus Christ, through John, reveals once again that Cain's offspring (the "Tares") are not truly the descendants of Jacob and Judah, but will lie and <u>claim</u> to be of Judah (Rev.2:9, 3:9):

> **And unto the angel of the church in Smyrna write; These things saith the first and the last, which was dead, and is alive;** (Rev.2:8)
>
> **I know thy works, and tribulation, and poverty, (but thou art rich) and I *know* the blasphemy of them <u>which say they are Jews, and are not</u>, but *are* the synagogue of Satan.** (Rev.2:9)

> **And to the angel of the church in Philadelphia write; These things saith he that is holy, he that is true, he that hath the key of David, he that openeth, and no man shutteth; and shutteth, and no man openeth;** (Rev.3:7)

I know thy works: behold, I have set before thee an open door, and no man can shut it: for thou hast a little strength, and hast kept my word, and hast not denied my name. (Rev.3:8)

Behold, I will make them of the synagogue of Satan, <u>which say they are Jews, and are not</u>, but do lie; behold, I will make them to come and worship before thy feet, and to know that I have loved thee. (Rev.3:9)

He that hath an ear, let him hear what the Spirit saith unto the churches. (Rev.3:13)

Chapter 3

Don't Eat, Don't Touch

The focus of this chapter is to find the distinction between two genealogies — the genealogy of Cain versus the genealogy of Adam. It will be helpful to first understand why God said to Adam in the Garden of Eden, "do not eat."

> **But of the tree of the knowledge of good and evil, thou shalt not eat of it: for in the day that thou eatest thereof thou shalt surely die.** (Gen.2:17)

To the prophet Ezekiel God said "eat."

> **But thou, son of man, hear what I say unto thee; Be not thou rebellious like that rebellious house: open thy mouth, and eat that I give thee.** (Ezk.2:8)
>
> **And when I looked, behold, an hand *was* sent unto me; and, lo, a roll of a book *was* therein;** (Ezk.2:9)

The word "eat" in the Bible was used figuratively for "listening and learning". It means we partake, absorb, digest, meditate upon, learn and understand. Therefore, what God says to the prophet Ezekiel was, "Listen to my word, listen to my instruction, understand it, meditate, digest, and absorb it."

Similarly, to the apostle John was commanded to "eat" the little book (the word of God):

> **And the voice which I heard from heaven spake unto me again, and said, Go *and* take the little book which is open in the hand of the angel which standeth upon the sea and upon the earth.** (Rev.10:8)
>
> **And I went unto the angel, and said unto him, Give me the little book. And he said unto me, Take *it*, and eat it up; and it shall make thy belly bitter, but it shall be in thy mouth sweet as honey.** (Rev.10:9)

The Lord Jesus Christ also said that whoever eats the Word of God shall live forever. As we have learned in chapter one, Jesus Christ is the living Word of God. The "bread" represents the Word of God which is the bread of life. As Jesus said:

> **I am the living bread which came down from heaven: if any man eat of this bread, he shall live for ever: and the bread that I will give is my flesh, which I will give for the life of the world.** (John 6:51)

It is unfortunate that, there are some (if not many) different interpretations of the word of God which causes much confusion. This makes it extremely difficult to understand and know the truth. Because of this confusion, it builds spiritual hunger — hunger for the bread of life (i.e., our spiritual food), hunger for the truth, hunger for the knowledge of the words of the LORD.

Is there a famine for hearing the words of God with understanding?

Behold, the days come, saith the Lord GOD, that I will send a famine in the land, not a famine of bread, nor a thirst for water, but of hearing the words of the LORD: (Amos 8:11)

Hence, the famine is of hearing (intelligently) the words of the LORD, the famine for the bread of life, hunger for the knowledge and understanding of the living Word of God.

Are we now living in the days spoken of by the prophet Amos? Spiritual starvation will lead people to become spiritually dead.

The Lord Jesus Christ said:

Every plant, which my heavenly Father hath not planted, shall be rooted up. (Matt.15:13)

Let them alone: they be blind leaders of the blind. And if the blind lead the blind, both shall fall into the ditch. (Matt.15:14)

Can the blind lead the blind? shall they not both fall into the ditch? (Lk.6:39)

Clearly, Jesus Christ is not referring to someone who is actually blind, because a physically blind person is skilled and capable to lead the way without visual sight. Jesus was talking about _spiritual_ blindness — meaning those that don't fully understand the words of the LORD — those that don't have the knowledge of the truth, i.e., the blind guides. The Pharisees were supposed to lead people to the kingdom of heaven; they were supposed to teach the word of God properly, and guide people to go through the "door," but instead they were blocking the only Way in. They were blocking the true door of heaven with their traditions and false teachings.

> **Making the word of God of none effect through your tradition, which ye have delivered: and many such like things do ye.** (Mk.7:13)

The blind guides have been causing the famine of spiritual food, which is the famine of the end time. Jesus said;

> **I am the door: by me if any man enter in, he shall be saved, and shall go in and out, and find pasture.** (John 10:9)

The door for the sheep was an illustration of Jesus Christ Himself, since there was only one door in to the sheepfold, and there is also only one way to obtain salvation and eternal life — that is through Christ Jesus. And whoever enters by that door will be saved, "and shall go in and out," meaning, they will have freedom, "and find pasture," that's the spiritual food. Spiritual food is the living Word of God, the truth, for the truth shall make you free (John 8:32).

> **But woe unto you, scribes and Pharisees, hypocrites! for ye shut up the kingdom of heaven against men: for ye neither go in *yourselves*, neither suffer ye them that are entering to go in.** (Matt.23:13)

With spiritual discernment, we should be able to determine if something is unrealistic; we either listen to it or not, it's our choice. The immortality of our own soul will depend on our own decision alone. So we should not listen to a blind guide, and *never* follow someone who is spiritually blind, or else we will end up being led into a ditch along with them.

> **He that hath an ear, let him hear what the Spirit saith unto the churches; To him that overcometh will I give to eat of the tree of life, which is in the midst of the paradise of God.** (Rev.2:7)

> **He that overcometh shall inherit all things; and I will be his God, and he shall be my son.** (Rev.21:7)

As we can see there's a condition for anyone to have the right to eat from the tree of life, and that is to be an overcomer. Hearing God's word with understanding and with the help of the Holy Spirit will help anyone overcome false teaching and deception of this world age.

> **Blessed *are* they that do his commandments, that they may have right to the tree of life, and may enter in through the gates into the city.** (Rev.22:14)

It is the same "tree of life" that was in the Garden of Eden. The tree of life is symbolic of the Lord Jesus Christ, the life giver. His fruit is good, and His spiritual food is everlasting life.

But there was another peculiar tree in the Garden of Eden which is the opposite of life. This tree was called "the tree of the knowledge of good and evil," and it is symbolic of Satan, the devil in his role as the Serpent, the life destroyer. His fruit is poisonous and will cause death. That is the reason why God said "don't eat" from the tree of the knowledge of good and evil, in other words, don't listen to Satan's word, don't partake of it. Stay away from him, and don't listen to his teaching. Unfortunately, Adam and Eve both died spiritually after they partook it:

> **But of the tree of the knowledge of good and evil, thou shalt not eat of it: for in the day that thou eatest thereof thou shalt surely die.** (Gen.2:17)
>
> **And when the woman saw that the tree *was* good for food, and that it *was* pleasant to the eyes, and a tree to be desired to make *one* wise, she took of the fruit thereof, and did eat, and gave also unto her husband with her; and he did eat.** (Gen.3:6)

The phrase "the knowledge of good and evil" implies full of wisdom and knowledge of everything, and the "tree" symbolizes of a person. Even God liken Himself to a tree, God Himself used this symbol to describe Himself in the book of Hosea, as a green fir tree, an evergreen tree. It symbolizes eternal life of the Spirit:

"**I *am* like a green fir tree. From me is thy fruit found.**" (Hos.14:8)

The "serpent" in the Garden of Eden is one of the many names, roles, titles, and descriptions for Satan. For instance, he was called the "dragon", the "old serpent", the "Devil" in the book of Revelation:

> **And the great dragon was cast out, that old serpent, called the Devil, and Satan, which deceiveth the whole world: he**

> was cast out into the earth, and his angels were cast out with him. (Rev.12:9)

> And he laid hold on the dragon, that old serpent, which is the Devil, and Satan, and bound him a thousand years, (Rev.20:2)

Satan was called "little horn" in the book of Daniel, where it mentioned the prophecy for the coming of the false Messiah before the end of this world age:

> I considered the horns, and, behold, there came up among them another little horn, before whom there were three of the first horns plucked up by the roots: and, behold, in this horn *were* eyes like the eyes of man, and a mouth speaking great things. (Dan.7:8)

> And out of one of them came forth a little horn, which waxed exceeding great, toward the south, and toward the east, and toward the pleasant *land*. (Dan.8:9)

Again, in the book of Revelation, Satan is called the "beast." The beast with two little horns like that of a lamb; imitating Jesus Christ (John 1:29 — Christ is the Lamb of God), but he is the dragon, the fake Christ. Satan will play the role of the Antichrist — the religious beast:

> And I beheld another beast coming up out of the earth; and he had two horns like a lamb, and he spake as a dragon. (Rev.13:11)

> ... If any man worship the beast and his image, and receive *his* mark in his forehead, or in his hand, (Rev.14:9)
>
> The same shall drink of the wine of the wrath of God, which is poured out without mixture into the cup of his indignation; and he shall be tormented with fire and brimstone in the presence of the holy angels, and in the presence of the Lamb: (Rev.14:10)

Satan was also called the king of Tyrus, before the foundation of the world (Ezk.28:12), then after the fall he was called the prince of Tyrus (Ezk.28:2). He was called Lucifer (Isa.14:12); the god of this world (2Cor.4:4); the enemy (Matt.13:39); the wicked one (Matt.13:19, 38; 1John 3:12); thief (John 10:10; 1Thess.5:2, 4); antichrist (1John 2:18); the tempter (Matt.4:3; 1Thess.3:5); the accuser (Rev.12:10); adversary the devil (1Peter 5:8); the son of perdition (2Thess.2:3); to name a few.

One should not let such names convince oneself that God would create such a horrible creature. It was actually the complete opposite. Satan was a model of perfection the day God created him. Not only was he full of wisdom, possessing superior and supernatural knowledge, he was also a very handsome and blameless celestial being — the perfection of beauty, and he was called the "king of Tyrus" before the foundation of the world. God appointed Satan to be one of the protectors (the anointed cherub that covereth) of the "Mercy Seat." Satan loved and served God; he was perfect, as he was described in the book of Ezekiel:

> Son of man, take up a lamentation upon the king of Tyrus, and say unto him, Thus saith the Lord GOD; Thou sealest up the sum, full of wisdom, and perfect in beauty. (Ezk.28:12)
>
> Thou hast been in Eden the garden of God; every precious stone *was* thy covering, the sardius, topaz, and the diamond, the beryl, the onyx, and the jasper, the sapphire, the emerald, and the carbuncle, and gold: the workmanship of thy tabrets and of thy pipes was prepared in thee in the day that thou wast created. (Ezk.28:13)
>
> Thou *art* the anointed cherub that covereth; and I have set thee *so*: thou wast upon the holy mountain of God; thou hast walked up and down in the midst of the stones of fire. (Ezk.28:14)

The word "covereth" was translated from the Hebrew word *cakak*; (Strong's Concordance #H5526); a primitive root; properly, to entwine as a screen; by implication, to fence in, cover over, (figuratively) protect.

> Thou *wast* perfect in thy ways from the day that thou wast created, till iniquity was found in thee. (Ezk.28:15)

Then Satan became prideful and covetous, and he began to covet God. He did not want to be a servant of God anymore, but he wanted to be served. He stopped loving God, he stopped worshipping God, and he wanted to be worshipped as God.

One of Satan's temptations to Jesus Christ in the wilderness was for Jesus to bow down and worship him:

> Again, the devil taketh him up into an exceeding high mountain, and sheweth him all the kingdoms of the world, and the glory of them; (Matt.4:8)
>
> And saith unto him, All these things will I give thee, if thou wilt fall down and worship me. (Matt.4:9)
>
> Then saith Jesus unto him, Get thee hence, Satan: for it is written, Thou shalt worship the Lord thy God, and him only shalt thou serve. (Matt.4:10)

Pride and covetousness were the causes of Satan's own fall. Pride was the sin of Satan and it cost him to be sentenced to death:

> By the multitude of thy merchandise they have filled the midst of thee with violence, and thou hast sinned: therefore I will cast thee as profane out of the mountain of God: and I will destroy thee, O covering cherub, from the midst of the stones of fire. (Ezk.28:16)
>
> Thine heart was lifted up because of thy beauty, thou hast corrupted thy wisdom by reason of thy brightness: I will cast thee to the ground, I will lay thee before kings, that they may behold thee. (Ezk.28:17)
>
> Thou hast defiled thy sanctuaries by the multitude of thine iniquities, by the iniquity of thy traffick; therefore will I bring forth a fire from the midst of thee, it shall devour thee, and I will bring thee to ashes upon the earth in the sight of all them that behold thee. (Ezk.28:18)

> All they that know thee among the people shall be astonished at thee: thou shalt be a terror, and never *shalt* thou *be* any more. (Ezk.28:19)

So, the king of Tyrus has been judged by Almighty God. Satan was already sentenced to hell, along with the angels that followed Satan. The angels that chose Satan are also going to hell with him — the angels (the "sons of God" of Gen.6:2) who left their heavenly place, came down to earth and married any one of the daughters of Adam that they chose, which is totally against the law of the living God:

> **And the angels which kept not their first estate, but left their own habitation, he hath reserved in everlasting chains under darkness unto the judgment of the great day.** (Jude 1:6)

Adam and Eve were pure without sin; they were without knowledge of evil. The tree of the knowledge of good and evil was the serpent — Satan the devil. He was more cunning than any living creature. However, Satan failed in an attempt to deceive Adam directly while he was alone in the garden. So the cunning and handsome celestial being Satan the devil in his role as the Serpent, stood in front of the woman in the Garden of Eden, initiating conversation to the woman with a question:

> **Now the serpent was more subtil than any beast of the field which the LORD God had made. And he said unto the**

> **woman, Yea, hath God said, Ye shall not eat of every tree of the garden?** (Gen.3:1)

Recall when God commanded them not to listen to Satan. But can the woman resist Satan? is she able to resist listening to the word of the "father of lies?" Is there any chance for the woman to resist the temptation from the "tempter?" It was unfortunate that Satan was adored by the woman in the Garden of Eden, she found him irresistible!

> **And when the woman saw that the tree *was* good for food, and that it *was* pleasant to the eyes, and a tree to be desired to make *one* wise, she took of the fruit thereof, and did eat, and gave also unto her husband with her; and he did eat.** (Gen.3:6)

With the newfound knowledge from Satan, the woman shared it with her husband and persuaded him to partake of it, so they were both indeed became spiritually dead. Again, "Can the blind lead the blind? shall they not both fall into the ditch?" (Lk.6:39).

This is what happens when a spiritually blind person tries to lead, or shares something he or she truly believes, while unaware that they're being deceived.

The woman in the Garden of Eden was simply deceived by Satan and lost her "spiritual virginity." She was blinded by the beautiful appearance and the cunning words of Satan. She believed and accepted the lies from the "father of lies" — the Devil.

Protecting our spiritual virginity is very important. Losing the spiritual virginity is what the Apostle Paul is deeply concerned about. Paul does not want anyone to be seduced by the Serpent as Eve was in the Garden of Eden, because Satan will play his role as the Antichrist before the Second Coming of Jesus Christ. As Paul said;

> ... **for I have espoused you to one husband, that I may present** *you as* **a chaste virgin to Christ.** (2Cor.11:2)
>
> **But I fear, lest by any means, as the serpent beguiled Eve through his subtilty, so your minds should be corrupted from the simplicity that is in Christ.** (2Cor.11:3)

So, Paul warned the people not to let false apostles deceive and mislead them with their false teaching;

> **For such** *are* **false apostles, deceitful workers, transforming** (*disguising*) **themselves into the apostles of Christ.** (2Cor.11:13)

The phrase "false apostles" was translated from the Greek word "*pseudapostolos*" (Strong's Concordance #G5570); a spurious apostle, i.e. pretended preacher: — false teacher.

The word "transforming/transformed" was translated from the Greek word "*metaschematizo*" (Strong's Concordance #G3345) and it means; to transfigure or disguise; figuratively, to apply (by accommodation): — transfer, transform (self).

> **And no marvel; for Satan himself is transformed** (*disguised*) **into an angel of light.** (2Cor.11:14)

Satan will be cast from heaven's containment out into this earth before the second coming of the Lord Jesus Christ. Satan the old serpent from the Garden of Eden will disguise himself as the light of the world. Satan will pretend that he is Christ, claiming to be the Savior of the world. Satan will come prosperously and peaceably. He will promise to solve all the problems of the world, and he will even promise peace on earth. As it is written, many will believe Satan's lies and will worship him, unaware that they are worshipping the devil, the spurious Messiah the Antichrist. Satan will deceive the whole world and will destroy many with "peace!"

> **And the great dragon was cast out, that old serpent, called the Devil, and Satan, which deceiveth the whole world: he was cast out into the earth, and his angels were cast out with him. (Rev.12:9)**
>
> **And through his policy also he shall cause craft to prosper in his hand; and he shall magnify *himself* in his heart, and by peace shall destroy many: ... (Dan.8:25)**
>
> **And all that dwell upon the earth shall worship him, whose names are not written in the book of life of the Lamb slain from the foundation of the world. (Rev.13:8)**
>
> **If any man have an ear, let him hear. (Rev.13:9)**

The Lord Jesus Christ is expecting a faithful virgin bride (spiritually speaking) when He returns for the wedding. Again, this is what the Apostle Paul was concerned about, and that is the reason why he warned the people about false apostles. As Jesus said,

> **But woe unto them that are with child, and to them that give suck, in those days! for there shall be great distress in the land, and wrath upon this people.** (Lk.21:23)

Woe to those that are "with child" when the Lord Jesus Christ (the bridegroom) returns for the wedding. Naturally Jesus was not talking about a literal child, because there is no sin for a woman having a child. But Jesus was talking about being "spiritually impregnated" by Satan — the Antichrist, meaning those that are deceived and seduced by the False Christ, because they are unaware that the False Christ will come first before the True Christ returns, they will worship the False Christ thinking that they are worshipping the True Christ Jesus.

Therefore, those that are "with child" are no longer fit to be His bride, because they have been unfaithful to the Lord Jesus Christ. They accepted the false Christ, who disguised as the light of the world, and the one who will claim and pretend to be the Savior of the world:

> **For, behold, the days are coming, in the which they shall say, Blessed *are* the barren, and the wombs that never bare, and the paps which never gave suck.** (Lk.23:29)

If it is possible, that's what the Apostle Paul wished for everyone, to be spiritually chaste virgin to one husband for the Lord and Savior Jesus the Christ. Having the knowledge of the truth and with the help from the Holy Spirit will help anyone to protect their own spiritual purity, and to overcome the deception of false apostles and the Antichrist.

From the teaching of the "Parable of the Ten Virgins," Jesus was letting people know, how to get into the kingdom of heaven, and how it is going to be just before His Second Coming.

The "bridegroom" is Jesus Christ Himself. The "ten virgins" represent Christians waiting for the Second Coming of Christ Jesus. Five of the virgins were "wise," meaning they fully understood and were well informed in the word of God; they have the knowledge of the truth. The other five virgins were "foolish," meaning they were unlearned of God's word. They don't have enough knowledge of God's word in their mind. They don't have enough "truth" which was symbolized by the "oil" — not enough of truth to know that there are two Christs. So, they don't truly know who the true Christ is, therefore, Jesus also said to the five foolish virgins — "I know you not."

Since the five unlearned (foolish) virgins do not have enough truth (oil), then they're spiritually in darkness — no oil — no light, and without light, they cannot see the truth. So they're spiritually blind and confused about the word of God, not capable to recognize the "fake" Christ. Having no knowledge of the situation, they will worship the first one that will appear at midnight, the one that will come in disguise claiming to be the light of the world. He will sell them lies, and the foolish virgins will buy them. The five foolish virgins indeed will be deceived by the fake Christ. Let us listen and learn from the teaching of Jesus Christ:

> **Then shall the kingdom of heaven be likened unto ten virgins, which took their lamps, and went forth to meet the bridegroom.** (Matt.25:1)
>
> **And five of them were wise, and five *were* foolish.** (Matt.25:2)
>
> **They that *were* foolish took their lamps, and took no oil with them:** (Matt.25:3)
>
> **But the wise took oil in their vessels with their lamps.** (Matt.25:4)
>
> **While the bridegroom tarried, they all slumbered and slept.** (Matt.25:5)
>
> **And at midnight there was a cry made, Behold, the bridegroom cometh; go ye out to meet him.** (Matt.25:6)
>
> **Then all those virgins arose, and trimmed their lamps.** (Matt.25:7)
>
> **And the foolish said unto the wise, Give us of your oil; for our lamps are gone out.** (Matt.25:8)
>
> **But the wise answered, saying, *Not so*; lest there be not enough for us and you: but go ye rather to them that sell, and buy for yourselves.** (Matt.25:9)
>
> **And while they went to buy, the bridegroom came; and they that were ready went in with him to the marriage: and the door was shut.** (Matt.25:10)

> **Afterward came also the other virgins, saying, Lord, Lord, open to us.** (Matt.25:11)
>
> **But he answered and said, Verily I say unto you, I know you not.** (Matt.25:12)

It will be a very terrifying moment on that day, for anyone that will be rejected by the true Christ. Therefore, make certain that we have enough "oil," in other words, to have enough knowledge of the "truth." It requires knowledge and precise understanding of God's Word for anyone to be part of the wedding party, and that is the kingdom of heaven.

As one can see, it is absolutely essential to have enough knowledge of God's Word, before the Second Advent transpires in order to be free from the rejection of the true Christ. God knows that many of His children are walking in darkness, which is solely why God sent His only begotten Son — the Light — the Truth. As Jesus said,

> **I am the light of the world: he that followeth me shall not walk in darkness, but shall have the light of life.** (John 8:12)
>
> **If ye continue in my word, *then* are ye my disciples indeed;** (John 8:31)
>
> **And ye shall know the truth, and the truth shall make you free.** (John 8:32)

The woman in the Garden of Eden knew exactly the two things that she must not have done, which was, "don't eat and don't touch." Don't eat from the tree of the knowledge of good and evil, and don't touch with the tree of the knowledge of good and evil. Simply put, don't have anything to do with Satan the devil, don't listen to Satan's word, don't accept his teaching. Don't mingle with him, don't have sexual relations with him:

> **But of the fruit of the tree which *is* in the midst of the garden, God hath said, Ye shall not eat of it, neither shall ye touch it, lest ye die.** (Gen.3:3)

The word "touch" in this verse is very important for us to know the meaning from the Hebrew language, so that we need not to wonder why God was suddenly talking about putting hatred between Satan's offspring and the woman's offspring:

> **And I will put enmity between thee and the woman, and between thy seed and her seed;** (Gen.3:15)

It will also help us to easily understand the "Parable of the Tares of the Field," because Jesus was explaining what happened in the Garden of Eden, that there are literal children of the wicked one, that is Satan:

> **The field is the world; the good seed are the children of the kingdom; but <u>the tares are the children of the wicked *one*</u>;** (Matt.13:38)

The word "touch" was translated from the Hebrew word "*naga*" (Strong's Concordance #H5060); and it means to touch, i.e. lay the hand upon (for any purpose; <u>euphemism, to lie with a woman</u>).

The same Hebrew word *naga* translated *touch*, that when God intervene, to protect the seed line through which Christ would be born from and did not allowed Abimelech king of Gerar *"touch"* Abraham's wife Sarah (Gen.20:6).

> **And Abraham journeyed from thence toward the south country, and dwelled between Kadesh and Shur, and sojourned in Gerar.** (Gen.20:1)
>
> **And Abraham said of Sarah his wife, She *is* my sister: and Abimelech king of Gerar sent, and took Sarah.** (Gen.20:2)
>
> **But God came to Abimelech in a dream by night, and said to him, Behold, thou *art but* a dead man, for the woman which thou hast taken; for she *is* a man's wife.** (Gen.20:3)
>
> **But Abimelech had not come near her: and he said, Lord, wilt thou slay also a righteous nation?** (Gen.20:4)
>
> **Said he not unto me, She *is* my sister? and she, even she herself said, He *is* my brother: in the integrity of my heart and innocency of my hands have I done this.** (Gen.20:5)
>
> **And God said unto him in a dream, Yea, I know that thou didst this in the integrity of thy heart; for I also withheld thee from sinning against me: therefore suffered I thee not to <u>touch</u> her.** (Gen.20:6)
>
> **Now therefore restore the man *his* wife; for he *is* a prophet, and he shall pray for thee, and thou shalt live: and if thou restore *her* not, know thou that thou shalt surely die, thou, and all that *are* thine.** (Gen.20:7)

Knowing the meaning of the Hebrew word *"naga"* will also help us to understand the reason why the Apostle John would say; Cain was the progeny of Satan.

Not as Cain, *who* was of that wicked one, and slew his brother. And wherefore slew he him? Because his own works were evil, and his brother's righteous. (1John 3:12)

The woman in the Garden of Eden did not overcome the temptation, the craftiness, and the irresistible beauty of Satan. He successfully seduced the woman, and she lost both of her spiritual and her physical virginity to Satan. Satan wants to keep it a secret, he does not want anyone to know what he did in the Garden of Eden, and he has been very successful so far, because many are still confused about the word of God, still confused about the children of the wicked one.

Again, the teaching of Jesus Christ explains it clearly in the Parable of the Tares of the Field (Matt.13:24-30, 36-43), that is the reason Jesus (Matt.12:34, 23:33) and John the Baptist (Matt.3:7) called them the children of the snakes. Jesus Christ also pointed out the descendants of Cain in the book of John (8:44) that their father is the devil, a murderer from the beginning.

"And Adam knew Eve his wife; and she conceived, and bare Cain," (Gen.4:1)

Keep in mind that, before Adam (*naga*) lay with his wife Eve, there had already been a conception that took place between Satan and Eve in the prior chapter (Gen.3:6). The result of that conception was Cain; God revealed the result of that conception in (Gen.3:15).

This is why Cain is not listed under Adam's genealogy, because Adam was not Cain's father. Cain's father was the wicked one, the devil (1John 3:12).

"And she again bare his brother Abel." (Gen.4:2)

The word "again" was translated from the Hebrew word "*yacaph*" (Strong's Concordance #H3254); and it means; to add or augment (often adverbial, to continue to do a thing).

So after she gave birth to Cain, she continued in labor and gave birth to Abel. Therefore, Cain and Abel were fraternal twins (two different fathers).

> **And Cain talked with Abel his brother: and it came to pass, when they were in the field, that Cain rose up against Abel his brother, and slew him.** (Gen.4:8)

Cain committed the crime of murder — the first murder recorded in the word of God. So God expelled Cain from Eden. After, Cain feared for his own life from the people outside of Eden — mankind that God created before Adam and Eve, which is the "Pre-Adamic" people (Gen.1:27 — "male and female created he them").

> **And Cain said unto the LORD, My punishment *is* greater than I can bear.** (Gen.4:13)

> **Behold, thou hast driven me out this day from the face of the earth; and from thy face shall I be hid; and I shall be a fugitive and a vagabond in the earth; and it shall come to pass, *that* every one that findeth me shall slay me.** (Gen.4:14)

Then Cain settled in the land of Nod. During his exile, he took a wife from the "Pre-Adamic" people, begat a son, and built a city, which he named the city after his son Enoch:

> **And Cain went out from the presence of the LORD, and dwelt in the land of Nod, on the east of Eden.** (Gen.4:16)
>
> **And Cain knew his wife; and she conceived, and bare Enoch: and he builded a city, and called the name of the city, after the name of his son, Enoch.** (Gen.4:17)

The following verses will show us the names of Cain's genealogy, and Enoch being the first "kenites" (sons of Cain):

> **And unto Enoch was born Irad: and Irad begat Mehujael: and Mehujael begat Methusael: and Methusael begat Lamech.** (Gen.4:18)
>
> **And Lamech took unto him two wives: the name of the one** *was* **Adah, and the name of the other Zillah.** (Gen.4:19)
>
> **And Adah bare Jabal: he was the father of such as dwell in tents, and** *of such as have* **cattle.** (Gen.4:20)
>
> **And his brother's name** *was* **Jubal: he was the father of all such as handle the harp and organ.** (Gen.4:21)
>
> **And Zillah, she also bare Tubalcain, an instructor of every artificer in brass and iron: and the sister of Tubalcain** *was* **Naamah.** (Gen.4:22)
>
> **And the families of the scribes which dwelt at Jabez; the Tirathites, the Shimeathites,** *and* **Suchathites. These** *are* **the**

> **Kenites that came of Hemath, the father of the house of Rechab.** (1Chron.2:55)
>
> **... Jehonadab the son of Rechab ...** (2Kings 10:15, 23) — (Jehonadab/Jonadab was the founder of the Rechabites).

Then the family of the Rechabites, who fled into the walled city of Jerusalem for protection, from Nebuchadnezzar king of Babylon, settled in Jerusalem, and became part of the tribe of Judah, that is, a citizen of the land of Judea.

> **The word which came unto Jeremiah from the LORD in the days of Jehoiakim the son of Josiah king of Judah, saying,** (Jer.35:1)
>
> **Go unto the house of the Rechabites, and speak unto them, and bring them into the house of the LORD, into one of the chambers, and give them wine to drink.** (Jer.35:2)
>
> **But they said, We will drink no wine: for Jonadab the son of Rechab our father commanded us, saying, Ye shall drink no wine,** *neither* **ye, nor your sons for ever:** (Jer.35:6)
>
> **Neither shall ye build house, nor sow seed, nor plant vineyard, nor have** *any*: **but all your days ye shall dwell in tents; that ye may live many days in the land where ye** *be* **strangers.** (Jer.35:7)
>
> **But it came to pass, when Nebuchadrezzar king of Babylon came up into the land, that we said, Come, and let us go to Jerusalem for fear of the army of the Chaldeans, and for fear of the army of the Syrians: <u>so we dwell at Jerusalem</u>.** (Jer.35:11)

They also managed to work their way into the position of scribes for Judah. They started to call themselves Jews, but keep in mind, they were the "Rechabites" (the sons of Cain), by residence they can claim to be Jew.

A similar case is just like the Apostle Paul. He was an Israelite from the tribe of Benjamin, a "Benjamite," and a Pharisee, raised and educated in the land of Judea. By residence, that made Paul a Jew. Also, Paul was a Roman citizen, because he was born in Tarsus, city of Cilicia. Paul was a free born Roman citizen. Unlike the chief captain had to pay a large sum for his citizenship. Therefore, by birth, Paul can claim to be Roman, and by residence, he can also claim to be a Jew. But neither was Paul's real identity, because he was from the tribe of Benjamin (not Judah). Let's listen to Paul:

> **I SAY then, Hath God cast away his people? God forbid. For I also am an Israelite, of the seed of Abraham, *of* the tribe of Benjamin.** (Rom.11:1)
>
> **I am verily a man *which am* a Jew, born in Tarsus, *a city* in Cilicia, yet brought up in this city at the feet of Gamaliel, *and* taught according to the perfect manner of the law of the fathers, and was zealous toward God, as ye all are this day.** (Acts 22:3)

> **And as they bound him with thongs, Paul said unto the centurion that stood by, Is it lawful for you to scourge a man that is a Roman, and uncondemned?** (Acts 22:25)
>
> **When the centurion heard *that*, he went and told the chief captain, saying, Take heed what thou doest: for this man is a Roman.** (Acts 22:26)
>
> **Then the chief captain came, and said unto him, Tell me, art thou a Roman? He said, Yea.** (Acts 22:27)
>
> **And the chief captain answered, With a great sum obtained I this freedom. And Paul said, But I was *free* born.** (Acts 22:28)

So it was the same situation for the Rechabites. Although they were not an Adamic people, and they were not the descendants of Jacob, nor were they of the tribe of Judah, but they can claim to be of Jews for they were a residence, or a born citizen of the land of Judea.

The people of the time Jesus Christ walked on earth, that Jesus called the children of snakes and that their father was the devil are the same people who questioned Jesus' authority, and the same people that falsely accused Jesus, and the same people that was responsible for the crucifixion, and consequently the death of the Lord Jesus the Christ.

There are two names in Adam's genealogy, that we need to pay special attention to avoid confusion, because their names are the same as the name of the sons of Cain. Obviously, they are two distinct people.

First, the name "Enoch" is the seventh from Adam and he was a prophet. This is not the Enoch of Cain's genealogy, who is the first Kenite:

> **And Enoch also, the seventh from Adam, prophesied of these, saying, Behold, the Lord cometh with ten thousands of his saints,** (Jude 1:14)

The second name is "Lamech." He was the son of Methuselah. This is not the son of Methusael, who was a Kenite.

A simple flow chart at the end of this chapter shows both the descendant of Cain and the descendant Adam. Hope it will help us see it more clearly. Abel's name was not included in the genealogy of Adam, because he was murdered by Cain. Abel did not have children of his own. So, no children — no genealogy.

The genealogy of Adam:

> **And Adam lived an hundred and thirty years, and begat *a son* in his own likeness, after his image; and called his name Seth:** (Gen.5:3)
>
> **And Seth lived an hundred and five years, and begat Enos:** (Gen.5:6)
>
> **And Enos lived ninety years, and begat Cainan:** (Gen.5:9)

And Cainan lived seventy years, and begat Mahalaleel: (Gen.5:12)

And Mahalaleel lived sixty and five years, and begat Jared: (Gen.5:15)

And Jared lived an hundred sixty and two years, and he begat Enoch: (Gen.5:18)

And Enoch lived sixty and five years, and begat Methuselah: (Gen.5:21)

And Methuselah lived an hundred eighty and seven years, and begat Lamech: (Gen.5:25)

And Lamech lived an hundred eighty and two years, and begat a son: (Gen.5:28)

And he called his name Noah, (Gen.5:29)

And Noah was five hundred years old: and Noah begat **Shem**, Ham, and Japheth. (Gen.5:32)

These *are* the generations of Shem: Shem *was* an hundred years old, and begat Arphaxad two years after the flood: (Gen.11:10)

And Arphaxad lived five and thirty years, and begat Salah: (Gen.11:12)

And Salah lived thirty years, and begat Eber: (Gen.11:14)

And Eber lived four and thirty years, and begat Peleg: (Gen.11:16)

And Peleg lived thirty years, and begat Reu: (Gen.11:18)

> And Reu lived two and thirty years, and begat Serug: (Gen.11:20)
>
> And Serug lived thirty years, and begat Nahor: (Gen.11:22)
>
> And Nahor lived nine and twenty years, and begat Terah: (Gen.11:24)
>
> And Terah lived seventy years, and begat <u>Abram</u>, Nahor, and Haran. (Gen.11:26)
>
> Abram; the same *is* Abraham. (1Chron.1:27)
>
> And Abraham begat Isaac. The sons of Isaac; Esau and Israel. (1Chron.1:34)

Israel is the name given to Jacob after his wrestling with the angel of the LORD:

> Thy name shall be called no more Jacob, but Israel: for as a prince hast thou power with God and with men, and hast prevailed. (Gen.32:28)
>
> These *are* the sons of Israel; Reuben, Simeon, Levi, and <u>Judah</u>, Issachar, and Zebulun, (1Chron.2:1)
>
> Dan, Joseph, and Benjamin, Naphtali, Gad, and Asher. (1Chron.2:2)

Then from Judah and so on down to Heli — the father of the virgin Mary that gave birth to Jesus. The father-in-law of Joseph, which is the husband of the Virgin Mary:

> And Jesus himself began to be about thirty years of age, being (as was supposed) the son of Joseph, which was *the son* of Heli, (Lk.3:23)

Joseph was not the natural son of Heli. Joseph was begotten by Jacob; the son of Matthan, the grandfather of Joseph:

> **And Eliud begat Eleazar; and Eleazar begat Matthan; and Matthan begat Jacob;** (Matt.1:15)
>
> **And Jacob begat Joseph the husband of Mary, of whom was born Jesus, who is called Christ.** (Matt.1:16)

From the Virgin Mary to the birth of the Lord Jesus Christ, the only begotten Son of God, the Savior of the world, the King of kings and Lord of lords:

> **Now the birth of Jesus Christ was on this wise: When as his mother Mary was espoused to Joseph, before they came together, she was found with child of the Holy Ghost.** (Matt.1:18)
>
> **Then Joseph her husband, being a just *man*, and not willing to make her a public example, was minded to put her away privily.** (Matt.1:19)
>
> **But while he thought on these things, behold, the angel of the Lord appeared unto him in a dream, saying, Joseph, thou son of David, fear not to take unto thee Mary thy wife: for that which is conceived in her is of the Holy Ghost.** (Matt.1:20)
>
> **And she shall bring forth a son, and thou shalt call his name JESUS: for he shall save his people from their sins.** (Matt.1:21)
>
> **Now all this was done, that it might be fulfilled which was spoken of the Lord by the prophet, saying,** (Matt.1:22)

Behold, a virgin shall be with child, and shall bring forth a son, and they shall call his name Emmanuel, which being interpreted is, God with us. (Matt.1:23)

88   Killer of the Christ

Simple flow chart showing the distinction between the two genealogies:

Chapter 4

The Conspiracy

> **Rejoice greatly, O daughter of Zion; shout, O daughter of Jerusalem: behold, thy King cometh unto thee: he *is* just, and having salvation; lowly, and riding upon an ass, and upon a colt the foal of an ass. (Zech.9:9)**

That was the first advent, and it foretells the first coming of Jesus Christ, the humble Messiah. He came to bring salvation to the world, and it is called the "crucifixion." His crucifixion on the cross opened salvation to all.

The first and the second advent of the Lord and Savior Jesus Christ was written in the book of prophet Zechariah. The following verse will be the second advent. That's when Jesus Christ returns, riding (not on a donkey but) on a white horse as King of kings and Lord of lords:

> **And I will cut off the chariot from Ephraim, and the horse from Jerusalem, and the battle bow shall be cut off: and he shall speak peace unto the heathen: and his dominion *shall be* from sea *even* to sea, and from the river *even* to the ends of the earth. (Zech.9:10)**

The first advent, of course, is already being fulfilled, and it is recorded in detail in the book of Matthew:

And when they drew nigh unto Jerusalem, and were come to Bethphage, unto the mount of Olives, then sent Jesus two disciples, (Matt.21:1)

Saying unto them, Go into the village over against you, and straightway ye shall find an ass tied, and a colt with her: loose *them*, and bring *them* unto me. (Matt.21:2)

And if any *man* say ought unto you, ye shall say, The Lord hath need of them; and straightway he will send them. (Matt.21:3)

All this was done, that it might be fulfilled which was spoken by the prophet, saying, (Matt.21:4)

Tell ye the daughter of Sion, Behold, thy King cometh unto thee, meek, and sitting upon an ass, and a colt the foal of an ass. (Matt.21:5)

And the disciples went, and did as Jesus commanded them, (Matt.21:6)

And brought the ass, and the colt, and put on them their clothes, and they set *him* thereon. (Matt.21:7)

And a very great multitude spread their garments in the way; others cut down branches from the trees, and strawed *them* in the way. (Matt.21:8)

And the multitudes that went before, and that followed, cried, saying, Hosanna to the Son of David: Blessed *is* he that cometh in the name of the Lord; Hosanna in the highest. (Matt.21:9)

> And when he was come into Jerusalem, all the city was moved, saying, Who is this? (Matt.21:10)
>
> And the multitude said, This is Jesus the prophet of Nazareth of Galilee. (Matt.21:11)

The prophet Isaiah also prophesied both advents of the Lord and Savior Jesus Christ:

> The Spirit of the Lord GOD *is* upon me; because the LORD hath anointed me to preach good tidings unto the meek; he hath sent me to bind up the brokenhearted, to proclaim liberty to the captives, and the opening of the prison to *them that are* bound; (Isa.61:1)
>
> To proclaim the acceptable year of the LORD, and the day of vengeance of our God; to comfort all that mourn; (Isa.61:2)

Jesus Himself proclaimed the first advent (only) of the Messiah was fulfilled. That is why while He was reading the scroll of the prophet Isaiah, Jesus stopped in the middle of the sentence of verse two (Isa.61:2). Christ did not read "and the day of vengeance of our God; to comfort all that mourn;" He did not finish reading the rest of verse two, and He closed the book (Lk.4:19–20). Because it refers to the future second coming of the Lord Jesus the Christ.

The "day of vengeance" does not come until the second advent. Christ Jesus will return not to be crucified again, but He will return as King of kings and Lord of lords, and He will rule righteously:

> And he came to Nazareth, where he had been brought up: and, as his custom was, he went into the synagogue on the sabbath day, and stood up for to read. (Lk.4:16)
>
> And there was delivered unto him the book of the prophet Esaias. And when he had opened the book, he found the place where it was written, (Lk.4:17)
>
> The Spirit of the Lord *is* upon me, because he hath anointed me to preach the gospel to the poor; he hath sent me to heal the brokenhearted, to preach deliverance to the captives, and recovering of sight to the blind, to set at liberty them that are bruised, (Lk.4:18)
>
> To preach the acceptable year of the Lord. (Lk.4:19)
>
> And he closed the book, and he gave *it* again to the minister, and sat down. And the eyes of all them that were in the synagogue were fastened on him. (Lk.4:20)
>
> And he began to say unto them, This day is this scripture fulfilled in your ears. (Lk.4:21)

Accomplishing the scriptures as it is written, Jesus preached the gospel of the kingdom of God. He continuously healed people physically and spiritually, even during Sabbath day, everywhere He traveled. Jesus healed every person He encountered who had disease and sickness. He cleansed the lepers, helped the blind to receive sight, the lame to walk, the deaf to hear. Jesus even raised the dead. He performed many miracles and drove out unclean spirits. The unclean spirits knew exactly who Jesus was, so they had to obey whatever He said — there was no need for Christ to introduce Himself. The unclean spirits even knew that it was not yet the "end time," as it was written in the book of Matthew:

> And when he was come to the other side into the country of the Gergesenes, there met him two possessed with devils, coming out of the tombs, exceeding fierce, so that no man might pass by that way. (Matt.8:28)
>
> And, behold, they cried out, saying, What have we to do with thee, Jesus, thou Son of God? art thou come hither to torment us before the time? (Matt.8:29)

All these things about Jesus spread rapidly throughout the region.

> Now after that John was put in prison, Jesus came into Galilee, preaching the gospel of the kingdom of God, (Mk.1:14)
>
> And saying, The time is fulfilled, and the kingdom of God is at hand: repent ye, and believe the gospel. (Mk.1:15)
>
> And they went into Capernaum; and straightway on the sabbath day he entered into the synagogue, and taught. (Mk.1:21)
>
> And they were astonished at his doctrine: for he taught them as one that had authority, and not as the scribes. (Mk.1:22)
>
> And there was in their synagogue a man with an unclean spirit; and he cried out, (Mk.1:23)

> Saying, Let *us* alone; what have we to do with thee, thou Jesus of Nazareth? art thou come to destroy us? I know thee who thou art, the Holy One of God. (Mk.1:24)
>
> And Jesus rebuked him, saying, Hold thy peace, and come out of him. (Mk.1:25)
>
> And when the unclean spirit had torn him, and cried with a loud voice, he came out of him. (Mk.1:26)
>
> And they were all amazed, insomuch that they questioned among themselves, saying, What thing is this? what new doctrine *is* this? for with authority commandeth he even the unclean spirits, and they do obey him. (Mk.1:27)
>
> And immediately his fame spread abroad throughout all the region round about Galilee. (Mk.1:28)

But the scribes and the Pharisees were very upset. They accused Christ for violating the Sabbath. As it is recorded in the book of Luke chapter 6 verse 10. Jesus simply told the man to stretch his arm out, and the man's arm was restored. He did not perform any of those so-called "healing." Jesus did not touch the man or anoint the man. Jesus simply said unto the man; "Stretch fort thy hand." So, the scribes and Pharisees could not accuse Jesus of doing the healing on the Sabbath day. And of course, that makes them very upset, again:

> And it came to pass also on another sabbath, that he entered into the synagogue and taught: and there was a man whose right hand was withered. (Lk.6:6)

> And the scribes and Pharisees watched him, whether he would heal on the sabbath day; that they might find an accusation against him. (Lk.6:7)
>
> But he knew their thoughts, and said to the man which had the withered hand, Rise up, and stand forth in the midst. And he arose and stood forth. (Lk.6:8)
>
> Then said Jesus unto them, I will ask you one thing; Is it lawful on the sabbath days to do good, or to do evil? to save life, or to destroy *it*? (Lk.6:9)
>
> And looking round about upon them all, he said unto the man, Stretch forth thy hand. And he did so: and his hand was restored whole as the other. (Lk.6:10)
>
> And they were filled with madness; and communed one with another what they might do to Jesus. (Lk.6:11)

Many believed Jesus Christ and glorified God, and many followed Him. However, some of the religious leaders were not happy because they are concerned about losing power and authority over the people. That is, the fear of losing their influence on the Roman government. They knew something needed to be done to stop the growing popularity of Jesus Christ before it is too late ... and that included murder. Bear in mind what Jesus said to some of them in the book of John 8:44 — that their father is the devil and the desire of their father they will do.

> Then many of the Jews which came to Mary, and had seen the things which Jesus did, believed on him. (John 11:45)
>
> But some of them went their ways to the Pharisees, and told them what things Jesus had done. (John 11:46)
>
> Then gathered the chief priests and the Pharisees a council, and said, What do we? for this man doeth many miracles. (John 11:47)
>
> If we let him thus alone, all *men* will believe on him: and the Romans shall come and take away both our place and nation. (John 11:48)

Take away "our place," that is the temple — the center and source of all their influence and power.

> And one of them, *named* Caiaphas, being the high priest that same year, said unto them, Ye know nothing at all, (John 11:49)
>
> Nor consider that it is expedient for us, that one man should die for the people, and that the whole nation perish not. (John 11:50)
>
> And this spake he not of himself: but being high priest that year, he prophesied that Jesus should die for that nation; (John 11:51)
>
> And not for that nation only, but that also he should gather together in one the children of God that were scattered abroad. (John 11:52)
>
> Then from that day forth they took counsel together for to put him to death. (John 11:53)

After the miracle of raising Lazarus from the dead by Jesus, the chief priests conspired to kill Lazarus as well. Perhaps it is a good time to remind ourselves again the teaching of Jesus Christ, that is, the Parable of the Tares — the Kenites (the sons of Cain). This was a very dangerous group of people, as they just don't care who they murder. They will try to eliminate anyone that gets in their way.

> **Then Jesus six days before the passover came to Bethany, where Lazarus was which had been dead, whom he raised from the dead.** (John 12:1)
>
> **Much people of the Jews therefore knew that he was there: and they came not for Jesus' sake only, but that they might see Lazarus also, whom he had raised from the dead.** (John 12:9)
>
> **But the chief priests consulted that they might put Lazarus also to death;** (John 12:10)
>
> **Because that by reason of him many of the Jews went away, and believed on Jesus.** (John 12:11)

Because of Lazarus' resurrection, many were convinced that this Jesus undoubtedly the Messiah, and many Jews withdrew from the chief priests and believed in Jesus the Christ.

The chief priests and the scribes wanted Jesus dead. But they feared how the people would react, because a great number of the people loved Jesus. They can't just simply kill Jesus themselves. So, they determined a way on how they might accuse Him of some crime which was, that they might deliver Him unto the Roman power and authority of the governor (Pontius Pilate) to be crucified to death. He alone had that authority, as Pilate said;

> **Then saith Pilate unto him, Speakest thou not unto me? knowest thou not that I have power to crucify thee, and have power to release thee?** (John 19:10)

Therefore; they tried to trap Jesus. They sent spies who pretended to be righteous men, and they asked questions hoping to catch Jesus of saying something that is against the law. The plot was to deliver Jesus over to the Roman authority of the governor. But Jesus knew what was in their hearts:

> **And the chief priests and the scribes the same hour sought to lay hands on him; and they feared the people: for they perceived that he had spoken this parable against them.** (Lk.20:19)

> **And they watched him, and sent forth spies, which should feign themselves just men, that they might take hold of his words, that so they might deliver him unto the power and authority of the governor.** (Lk.20:20)

> **And they asked him, saying, Master, we know that thou sayest and teachest rightly, neither acceptest thou the person of any, but teachest the way of God truly:** (Lk.20:21)

> **Is it lawful for us to give tribute unto Caesar, or no?** (Lk.20:22)

But he perceived their craftiness, and said unto them, Why tempt ye me? (Lk.20:23)

Shew me a penny. Whose image and superscription hath it? They answered and said, Caesar's. (Lk.20:24)

And he said unto them, Render therefore unto Caesar the things which be Caesar's, and unto God the things which be God's. (Lk.20:25)

What Jesus is saying is to obey the law of the land, pay your taxes that belongs to Caesar. But in front of Pontius Pilate they accused Jesus of saying the opposite;

And they began to accuse him, saying, We found this *fellow* perverting the nation, and forbidding to give tribute to Caesar, saying that he himself is Christ a King. (Lk.23:2)

Jesus said to render unto God the things which be God's. What is it then that belongs to God? In the book of Ezekiel, God said; "Behold, all souls are mine;" (Ezk.18:4) We all belong to Almighty God.

Almighty God is the creator and owner of all things, and He is in control of all things. However, the one thing God will not control is the feelings of His children toward Him. God will not force anybody to love Him. Whether they will love Him or not, God gave His children that freedom to choose. The Heavenly Father wants true love from His children:

For I desired mercy, and not sacrifice; and the knowledge of God more than burnt offerings. (Hosea 6:6)

God Almighty wants loving-kindness (mercy) from His children, and He wants His children to have the knowledge of God. To love God enough that one will listen to Him, and seek knowledge concerning the LORD, so that they (the souls) may inherit everlasting life and be with the Father forever.

The other plot they had was to take Jesus in quietly, without the danger of an uproar among the people, and have Him put to death. We were told in the book of Luke that;

> **Then entered Satan into Judas surnamed Iscariot, being of the number of the twelve.** (Lk.22:3).

Then Judas Iscariot helped them accomplished their plot; "I will deliver him unto you" Judas said unto them (Matt.26:15). Judas offered his service to the chief priests. What Judas is saying is "I know exactly where to find Jesus, and I know when and how to capture Him. This is when there's not a lot of people around, when most of the people were in their beds, so there would be no danger of opposition and avoid uproar among the people."

> **Then assembled together the chief priests, and the scribes, and the elders of the people, unto the palace of the high priest, who was called Caiaphas,** (Matt.26:3)
>
> **And consulted that they might take Jesus by subtilty, and kill him.** (Matt.26:4)
>
> **But they said, Not on the feast** *day***, lest there be an uproar among the people.** (Matt.26:5)

> **Then one of the twelve, called Judas Iscariot, went unto the chief priests,** (Matt.26:14)
>
> **And said *unto them*, What will ye give me, and I will deliver him unto you? And they covenanted with him for thirty pieces of silver.** (Matt.26:15)
>
> **And from that time he sought opportunity to betray him.** (Matt.26:16)

It was the kiss of betrayal as Jesus said, "Judas, betrayest thou the Son of man with a kiss?" (Lk.22:48) Judas Iscariot identified Jesus with a kiss to a large mob working for the chief priests and elders. Then Jesus was quickly seized and taken into custody:

> **And while he yet spake, lo, Judas, one of the twelve, came, and with him a great multitude with swords and staves, from the chief priests and elders of the people.** (Matt.26:47)
>
> **Now he that betrayed him gave them a sign, saying, Whomsoever I shall kiss, that same is he: hold him fast.** (Matt.26:48)
>
> **And forthwith he came to Jesus, and said, Hail, master; and kissed him.** (Matt.26:49)
>
> **And Jesus said unto him, Friend, wherefore art thou come? Then came they, and laid hands on Jesus, and took him.** (Matt.26:50)

Then they started to look for false witnesses, to lie and slander Jesus Christ. They wanted someone to falsely accuse Him, to secure false evidence against Jesus to have him put to death.

> And they that had laid hold on Jesus led *him* away to Caiaphas the high priest, where the scribes and the elders were assembled. (Matt.26:57)
>
> Now the chief priests, and elders, and all the council, sought false witness against Jesus, to put him to death; (Matt.26:59)

Did they pay these false witnesses? And the people they persuaded, that cried out "crucify him," did they pay them also? They did pay Judas Iscariot, and they also did later pay the soldiers that guarded the tomb of Jesus Christ. They instructed them what to say and to lie for them, as it is written in the book of Matthew chapter 28 verses 12 and 13; "they gave large money unto the soldiers, Saying, Say ye, His disciples came by night, and stole him *away* while we slept." Obviously, it's another lie, because if they were sleeping, how then can they tell who came or what happened?

> But found none: yea, though many false witnesses came, *yet* found they none. At the last came two false witnesses, (Matt.26:60)

Even though many false witnesses came forward, they did not find any, because the false witnesses had a little bit of conflict between the two statement of complaint. Both of their testimonies did not agree with one another. In other words, they could not get their lies straight (under the law they must have two witnesses). And finally came two false witnesses;

> And said, This fellow said, I am able to destroy the temple of God, and to build it in three days. (Matt.26:61)

So, did Jesus say that He can destroy the temple of God and build it in three days? Certainly, it was false. That was not what Jesus said. Let's find out what exactly Jesus said in the book of John:

> **Jesus answered and said unto them, Destroy this temple, and in three days I will raise it up.** (John 2:19)

In other words, you (not "I" but "you") destroy this temple and I will raise it up in three days.

> **Then said the Jews, Forty and six years was this temple in building, and wilt thou rear it up in three days?** (John 2:20)
>
> **But he spake of the temple of his body.** (John 2:21)

Jesus was not even talking about the physical structure of the building of the temple, but He was talking about His own body. In other words, what Jesus is saying; "You destroy (crucify) Me, and after three days I will rise again!"

> **When therefore he was risen from the dead, his disciples remembered that he had said this unto them; and they believed the scripture, and the word which Jesus had said.** (John 2:22)

In the book of Revelation, it tells us about the temple in the eternity:

> **And I saw no temple therein: for the Lord God Almighty and the Lamb are the temple of it.** (Rev.21:22)

Unfortunately, the people misunderstood what He was saying, and believed the lies of the two false witnesses instead. As it is written in the book of Matthew, while Jesus was on the cross;

> And they that passed by reviled him, wagging their heads, (Matt.27:39)
>
> And saying, Thou that destroyest the temple, and buildest *it* in three days, save thyself. If thou be the Son of God, come down from the cross. (Matt.27:40)

With the support of false witnesses, they falsely and unjustly accused Jesus of blasphemy. Then they managed to have the judgment result in a guilty death sentence.

> And the high priest arose, and said unto him, Answerest thou nothing? what *is it* which these witness against thee? (Matt.26:62)
>
> But Jesus held his peace. And the high priest answered and said unto him, I adjure thee by the living God, that thou tell us whether thou be the Christ, the Son of God. (Matt.26:63)
>
> Jesus saith unto him, Thou hast said: nevertheless I say unto you, Hereafter shall ye see the Son of man sitting on the right hand of power, and coming in the clouds of heaven. (Matt.26:64)
>
> Then the high priest rent his clothes, saying, He hath spoken blasphemy; what further need have we of witnesses? behold, now ye have heard his blasphemy. (Matt.26:65)
>
> What think ye? They answered and said, He is guilty of death. (Matt.26:66)

Furthermore, early in the morning another counsel is held for another conspiracy how to kill Jesus the Christ. They would need to have the Roman government's approval, and Pontius Pilate the Roman governor would have to pass the sentence. So this is what they set after.

> **When the morning was come, all the chief priests and elders of the people took counsel against Jesus to put him to death:** (Matt.27:1)
>
> **And when they had bound him, they led *him* away, and delivered him to Pontius Pilate the governor.** (Matt.27:2)

The reason why they need to deliver Jesus to Pontius Pilate the governor was because they do not have the power of capital punishment. They could religiously convict someone to death, but they did not have the authority to do the crucifixion. They could put no man to death, as it is written in the book of John chapter 18. So, they needed Pontius Pilate's authority to execute the sentence they had passed upon Jesus:

> **Then said Pilate unto them, Take ye him, and judge him according to your law. The Jews therefore said unto him, It is not lawful for us to put any man to death:** (John 18:31)

So when they deliver Jesus to Pilate the governor, naturally they must lie against Jesus. Their only move is to falsely accuse Him, and they are skilled at it. They told Pilate that Jesus is an evildoer, a lawbreaker, a trouble maker, telling people not to pay tribute to Caesar and claimed to be a king himself that prompted Pilate to ask Jesus if He is a king. All they needed to do this time is to convince Pontius Pilate the Roman governor, that Jesus deserves the death penalty, of course, by their lies and false accusations.

> **Then led they Jesus from Caiaphas unto the hall of judgment: and it was early; and they themselves went not into the judgment hall, lest they should be defiled; but that they might eat the passover.** (John 18:28)
>
> **Pilate then went out unto them, and said, What accusation bring ye against this man?** (John 18:29)
>
> **They answered and said unto him, If he were not a malefactor, we would not have delivered him up unto thee.** (John 18:30)
>
> **Then said Pilate unto them, Take ye him, and judge him according to your law. The Jews therefore said unto him, It is not lawful for us to put any man to death:** (John 18:31)
>
> **That the saying of Jesus might be fulfilled, which he spake, signifying what death he should die.** (John 18:32)
>
> **Then Pilate entered into the judgment hall again, and called Jesus, and said unto him, Art thou the King of the Jews?** (John 18:33)
>
> **Jesus answered him, Sayest thou this thing of thyself, or did others tell it thee of me?** (John 18:34)

After Pilate examined Jesus, he found no fault, and decided to release Him, since Jesus is an innocent righteous man. As Judas Iscariot said; "I have sinned in that I have betrayed the innocent blood" (Matt.27:4). Pontius Pilate's wife also sent him this message while he was sitting on the judgment seat; "Have thou nothing to do with that just man" (Matt.27:19). And Pontius Pilate himself publicly declared Jesus is innocent; "saying, I am innocent of the blood of this just person" (Matt.27:24). Herod also agreed and confirmed the innocence of Jesus Christ (Lk.23:15). Even one of the malefactors said while still hanging on the cross; "this man hath done nothing amiss" (Lk.23:41).

> **And Pilate, when he had called together the chief priests and the rulers and the people,** (Lk.23:13)
>
> **Said unto them, Ye have brought this man unto me, as one that perverteth the people: and, behold, I, having examined *him* before you, have found no fault in this man touching those things whereof ye accuse him:** (Lk.23:14)
>
> **No, nor yet Herod: for I sent you to him; and, lo, nothing worthy of death is done unto him.** (Lk.23:15)
>
> **I will therefore chastise him, and release him.** (Lk.23:16)

Pontius Pilate tried at least three times to release Jesus;

> **Pilate therefore, willing to release Jesus, spake again to them.** (Lk.23:20)
>
> **But they cried, saying, Crucify *him*, crucify him.** (Lk.23:21)
>
> **And he said unto them the third time, Why, what evil hath he done? I have found no cause of death in him: I will therefore chastise him, and let *him* go.** (Lk.23:22)

This of course goes against what they wanted to accomplish. It goes against their plot to kill Jesus Christ and they were more furious than ever to get Jesus crucified. So they (the sons of Cain) put Pilate in a very difficult situation when they threatened him saying,

> **If thou let this man go, thou art not Caesar's friend: whosoever maketh himself a king speaketh against Caesar.** (John 19:12)

Pilate was alarmed when he heard their threat and accusation against him of treason. He was concerned about the chief priests and the elders of leading the uproar among the people. Because as a Roman governor, one of Pilate's responsibilities is to keep things in order, keeping peace in the community was the top priority.

If Pilate released Jesus, they would accuse him of treason against Caesar. But if Pilate executed their death sentence to Jesus, Pilate will not have a clear conscience, knowing that he put an innocent man to death. That is why Pilate "took water, and washed *his* hands before the multitude, saying, I am innocent of the blood of this just person." (Matt.27:24) Pilate just did not want to have any part of what was going on. Denying any responsibility for crucifying a completely innocent man.

But to the Kenites (sons of Cain), they simply do not care. They got what they wanted — to kill Jesus Christ. Obviously, it is not a problem for them to kill an innocent man. They took full responsibility for the innocent blood of Jesus Christ, for they said; "His blood *be* on us, and on our children" (Matt.27:25).

Bear in mind that it is referencing the sons of Cain. They are just like their father. As it is known that Cain murdered righteous Abel — the first murderer recorded in the Bible. Remember who Jesus said these people are in the book of John chapter 8 verse 44:

> **Ye are of *your* father the devil, and the lusts of your father ye will do. He was a murderer from the beginning, and abode not in the truth, because there is no truth in him. When he speaketh a lie, he speaketh of his own: for he is a liar, and the father of it.**

Jesus is letting us know who these people are again in the following verses recorded in the book of Matthew. And they admitted that they are sons of those who killed the prophets:

> **Woe unto you, scribes and Pharisees, hypocrites! because ye build the tombs of the prophets, and garnish the sepulchres of the righteous,** (Matt.23:29)

> **And say, If we had been in the days of our fathers, we would not have been partakers with them in the blood of the prophets.** (Matt.23:30)

> **Wherefore ye be witnesses unto yourselves, that ye are the children of them which killed the prophets.** (Matt.23:31)

> **Fill ye up then the measure of your fathers.** (Matt.23:32)

> **Ye serpents, *ye* generation of vipers, how can ye escape the damnation of hell?** (Matt.23:33)

Now at the feast (Passover), it was customary that Pilate would release one prisoner to the people (perhaps for political reason). Pilate was hoping that the crowd would choose Jesus. For he knew that the high priests had handed Jesus over out of jealousy — Matt.27:18. It is important to note that Barabbas was not the people's choice, but the chief priests and the elders with their authority persuaded the crowd to ask for Barabbas — Matt.27:20. For the regular folks who witnessed Jesus perform miracle after miracle and listened to His teachings, they struggled crying out to crucify such an extraordinary man:

> **Now at *that* feast the governor was wont to release unto the people a prisoner, whom they would.** (Matt.27:15)
>
> **And they had then a notable prisoner, called Barabbas.** (Matt.27:16)
>
> **Therefore when they were gathered together, Pilate said unto them, Whom will ye that I release unto you? Barabbas, or Jesus which is called Christ?** (Matt.27:17)
>
> **For he knew that for envy they had delivered him.** (Matt.27:18)
>
> **When he was set down on the judgment seat, his wife sent unto him, saying, Have thou nothing to do with that just man: for I have suffered many things this day in a dream because of him.** (Matt.27:19)

> But the chief priests and elders persuaded the multitude that they should ask Barabbas, and destroy Jesus. (Matt.27:20)
>
> The governor answered and said unto them, Whether of the twain will ye that I release unto you? They said, Barabbas. (Matt.27:21)
>
> Pilate saith unto them, What shall I do then with Jesus which is called Christ? *They* all say unto him, Let him be crucified. (Matt.27:22)
>
> And the governor said, Why, what evil hath he done? But they cried out the more, saying, Let him be crucified. (Matt.27:23)
>
> When Pilate saw that he could prevail nothing, but *that* rather a tumult was made, he took water, and washed *his* hands before the multitude, saying, I am innocent of the blood of this just person: see ye to *it*. (Matt.27:24)
>
> Then answered all the people, and said, His blood *be* on us, and on our children. (Matt.27:25)
>
> Then released he Barabbas unto them: and when he had scourged Jesus, he delivered *him* to be crucified. (Matt.27:26)

Pontius Pilate did try all in his power to release Jesus, but he failed. He had no choice but to give what the sons of Cain wanted — to crucify Jesus the Christ.

The chief priests and the Pharisees wanted to make sure that they had accomplished their mission of killing Jesus Christ. So they assigned their temple guard to watch the tomb:

> **Now the next day, that followed the day of the preparation, the chief priests and Pharisees came together unto Pilate,** (Matt.27:62)
>
> **Saying, Sir, we remember that that deceiver said, while he was yet alive, After three days I will rise again.** (Matt.27:63)
>
> **Command therefore that the sepulchre be made sure until the third day, lest his disciples come by night, and steal him away, and say unto the people, He is risen from the dead: so the last error shall be worse than the first.** (Matt.27:64)
>
> **Pilate said unto them, Ye have a watch: go your way, make** *it* **as sure as ye can.** (Matt.27:65)
>
> **So they went, and made the sepulchre sure, sealing the stone, and setting a watch.** (Matt.27:66)

It is because they understood what Jesus said when they asked for a sign. Jesus told them that the only sign given unto them is the sign of the prophet Jonas (or Jonah):

> **Then certain of the scribes and of the Pharisees answered, saying, Master, we would see a sign from thee.** (Matt.12:38)
>
> **But he answered and said unto them, An evil and adulterous generation seeketh after a sign; and there shall no sign be given to it, but the sign of the prophet Jonas:** (Matt.12:39)

> For as Jonas was three days and three nights in the whale's belly; so shall the Son of man be three days and three nights in the heart of the earth. (Matt.12:40)

Jesus also privately foretold His disciples what is going to transpire when they arrive in Jerusalem. Three days after the crucifixion, He is going to resurrect. The disciples did not quite understand what Jesus meant, and it seemed like they would forget about it after the crucifixion:

> And Jesus going up to Jerusalem took the twelve disciples apart in the way, and said unto them, (Matt.20:17)
>
> Behold, we go up to Jerusalem; and the Son of man shall be betrayed unto the chief priests and unto the scribes, and they shall condemn him to death, (Matt.20:18)
>
> And shall deliver him to the Gentiles to mock, and to scourge, and to crucify *him*: and the third day he shall rise again. (Matt.20:19)
>
> When therefore he was risen from the dead, his disciples remembered that he had said this unto them; and they believed the scripture, and the word which Jesus had said. (John 2:22)

And surely three days after the crucifixion, the guards reported their terrifying experience to the chief priests. They realized that Jesus was resurrected exactly as He told them. The tomb was empty. Now the chief priests and the elders held counsel again. They bribed the guards to lie for them and instructed them to say that Jesus' body was stolen by His disciples while they were asleep (again, how can the guards know that it was Jesus' disciples that stole the body if they were sleeping?).

> **In the end of the sabbath, as it began to dawn toward the first *day* of the week, came Mary Magdalene and the other Mary to see the sepulchre.** (Matt.28:1)
>
> **And, behold, there was a great earthquake: for the angel of the Lord descended from heaven, and came and rolled back the stone from the door, and sat upon it.** (Matt.28:2)
>
> **His countenance was like lightning, and his raiment white as snow:** (Matt.28:3)
>
> **And for fear of him the keepers did shake, and became as dead *men*.** (Matt.28:4)
>
> **And the angel answered and said unto the women, Fear not ye: for I know that ye seek Jesus, which was crucified.** (Matt.28:5)
>
> **He is not here: for he is risen, as he said. Come, see the place where the Lord lay.** (Matt.28:6)
>
> **And go quickly, and tell his disciples that he is risen from the dead; and, behold, he goeth before you into Galilee; there shall ye see him: lo, I have told you.** (Matt.28:7)
>
> **And they departed quickly from the sepulchre with fear and great joy; and did run to bring his disciples word.** (Matt.28:8)
>
> **And as they went to tell his disciples, behold, Jesus met them, saying, All hail. And they came and held him by the feet, and worshipped him.** (Matt.28:9)

> Then said Jesus unto them, Be not afraid: go tell my brethren that they go into Galilee, and there shall they see me. (Matt.28:10)
>
> Now when they were going, behold, some of the watch came into the city, and shewed unto the chief priests all the things that were done. (Matt.28:11)
>
> And when they were assembled with the elders, and had taken counsel, they gave large money unto the soldiers, (Matt.28:12)
>
> Saying, Say ye, His disciples came by night, and stole him *away* while we slept. (Matt.28:13)
>
> And if this come to the governor's ears, we will persuade him, and secure you. (Matt.28:14)
>
> So they took the money, and did as they were taught: and this saying is commonly reported among the Jews until this day. (Matt.28:15)

Through conspiracy, lies, false witnesses, false accusations, bribes, stirring up the crowd, and so forth, they managed to nail Christ's heel on the cross, and that fulfilled the first prophecy of the Bible concerning the sons of Cain (Gen.3:15). The Bible foretold the killer of the Christ from the beginning.

The conspiracy by the sons of Cain for nailing Christ's heel on the cross just fulfilled God's plan of eternal salvation, even though they may not realize it. As Christ said,

> **Think not that I am come to destroy the law, or the prophets: I am not come to destroy, but to fulfil.** (Matt.5:17)

While they were eating (known as the Last Supper);

> **And he took the cup, and gave thanks, and gave *it* to them, saying, Drink ye all of it;** (Matt.26:27)

> **For this is my blood of the new testament, which is shed for many for the remission of sins.** (Matt.26:28)

The crucifixion of Christ brought the ceremonial law of the old testament to an end, so they were no longer necessary. Christ fulfilled them (Matt.5:17), and they were nailed to His cross. Christ;

> **Blotting out the handwriting of ordinances that was against us, which was contrary to us, and took it out of the way, nailing it to his cross;** (Col.2:14)

> ***And* having spoiled principalities and powers, he made a shew of them openly, triumphing over them in it.** (Col.2:15)

And as it is written, Christ died on the cross, so that he might destroy him who had the power of death (that is to say, the devil):

> **Forasmuch then as the children are partakers of flesh and blood, he also himself likewise took part of the same; that through death he might destroy him that had the power of death, that is, the devil;** (Heb.2:14).

Christ paid that price on the cross so that we can have forgiveness of sin and obtain eternal life. Christ had no sin. He was the perfect sacrifice. The blood of Jesus the Christ on the cross forgives sin, if people sincerely ask God for forgiveness and repent.

As we have learned from the previous chapter (ch.1), it is not possible to find salvation through human effort of trying to follow all the laws. Sooner or later everybody will break those laws. The law was not able to give eternal life.

Before the crucifixion of Jesus Christ, there was no eternal salvation. Before Christ paid the price on the cross, people lived in the dispensation that was covered by the law of God. People had to do it by the law. By the law almost everything is cleansed with blood. If there was no blood shed, then there was no forgiveness of sins. The law will help people keep out of trouble, however the blood of bulls and goats cannot possibly remove sins, it was only an annual reminder of sins. Let's listen to the teachings of Apostle Paul:

> **And almost all things are by the law purged with blood; and without shedding of blood is no remission.** (Heb.9:22)
>
> **But in those *sacrifices there is* a remembrance again *made* of sins every year.** (Heb.10:3)
>
> **For *it is* not possible that the blood of bulls and of goats should take away sins.** (Heb.10:4)

After the crucifixion of Jesus Christ and through the blood that Christ shed on the cross, we now can be cleansed. The blood of Jesus Christ brought about the new covenant. We now live in a dispensation of God's grace. By faith and belief on the Lord Jesus the Christ, people can receive God's promise of eternal life:

> **And being made perfect, he became the author of eternal salvation unto all them that obey him;** (Heb.5:9)
>
> **In whom we have redemption through his blood, the forgiveness of sins, according to the riches of his grace;** (Eph.1:7)
>
> **For by grace are ye saved through faith; and that not of yourselves:** *it is* **the gift of God:** (Eph.2:8)
>
> **Not of works, lest any man should boast.** (Eph.2:9)
>
> **But before faith came, we were kept under the law, shut up unto the faith which should afterwards be revealed.** (Gal.3:23)
>
> **Wherefore the law was our schoolmaster** *to bring us* **unto Christ, that we might be justified by faith.** (Gal.3:24)

Jesus last word on the cross, "It is finished" (John 19:30). Christ accomplished and fulfilled all the scriptures as it is written for the first Advent. Then He bowed His head and gave up the Spirit.

The death and the resurrection of Jesus the Christ accomplished all things. Through the blood of Christ provided salvation for all mankind, making it possible for everyone who believes in Him to have eternal life instead of perishing.

Christ's blood on the cross gave people a new beginning. So whenever a person sincerely asks God for forgiveness and repented in the name of His only begotten Son Jesus the Christ, they become a new creation. We have the new testament which has fulfilled the old, and we have that new testament in Christ.

> **Therefore if any man *be* in Christ, *he is* a new creature: old things are passed away; behold, all things are become new.** (2Cor.5:17)
>
> **As ye have therefore received Christ Jesus the Lord, *so* walk ye in him:** (Col.2:6)
>
> **Rooted and built up in him, and stablished in the faith, as ye have been taught, abounding therein with thanksgiving.** (Col.2:7)

However, Apostle Paul warned people not to be led astray: avoid those who cause division, cause people to stumble through their false doctrine, and those that follow the traditions of men that make void the word of God:

> **Beware lest any man spoil you through philosophy and vain deceit, after the tradition of men, after the rudiments of the world, and not after Christ.** (Col.2:8)
>
> **Now I beseech you, brethren, mark them which cause divisions and offences contrary to the doctrine which ye have learned; and avoid them.** (Rom.16:17)

> **For they that are such serve not our Lord Jesus Christ, but their own belly; and by good words and fair speeches deceive the hearts of the simple.** (Rom.16:18)

Apostle Paul advised to diligently search and study the word of God, so that God can utilize you to bring others to His truth. Let God see that at least as a workman, having no cause to be ashamed of the way you handle the word of God, by rightly dividing the word of the Truth:

> **Study to shew thyself approved unto God, a workman that needeth not to be ashamed, rightly dividing the word of truth.** (2Tim.2:15)

> **And the God of peace shall bruise Satan under your feet shortly. The grace of our Lord Jesus Christ** *be* **with you. Amen.** (Rom.16:20)

Chapter 5

The Day of Vengeance

The first advent of Jesus Christ was the saving grace of Almighty God. Christ shed blood for the remission of sins (Matt.26:28), so that everyone who believes in Him may have eternal life — we are still living in that dispensation of grace:

> "**That whosoever believeth in him should not perish, but have eternal life.**" (John 3:15)

However, this present dispensation of God's grace will end at the second advent of our Lord Jesus the Christ. This second advent, Jesus will return as the avenger of the blood, and to restore everything in order. As God Almighty said:

> **To me *belongeth* vengeance, and recompence; their foot shall slide in *due* time: for the day of their calamity *is* at hand, and the things that shall come upon them make haste.** (Deut.32:35)

This will come to pass on the first day of the millennium year, fulfilling the second part of Isaiah's prophecy — "and the day of vengeance of our God; to comfort all that mourn;" (Isa.61:2). This future dispensation of time is the thousand years described in the book of Revelation:

> **And I saw an angel come down from heaven, having the key of the bottomless pit and a great chain in his hand.** (Rev.20:1)

> And he laid hold on the dragon, that old serpent, which is the Devil, and Satan, and bound him a thousand years, (Rev.20:2)
>
> And cast him into the bottomless pit, and shut him up, and set a seal upon him, that he should deceive the nations no more, till the thousand years should be fulfilled: and after that he must be loosed a little season. (Rev.20:3)
>
> And I saw thrones, and they sat upon them, and judgment was given unto them: and I *saw* the souls of them that were beheaded for the witness of Jesus, and for the word of God, and which had not worshipped the beast, neither his image, neither had received *his* mark upon their foreheads, or in their hands; and they lived and reigned with Christ a thousand years. (Rev.20:4)

Abel, who was murdered by his brother Cain, cried to God for his blood to be avenged. God said to Cain, "… the voice of thy brother's blood crieth unto me from the ground." (Gen.4:10)

Those who were slain by the enemy of God, were also crying for vengeance of their blood:

> And when he had opened the fifth seal, I saw under the altar the souls of them that were slain for the word of God, and for the testimony which they held: (Rev.6:9)
>
> And they cried with a loud voice, saying, How long, O Lord, holy and true, dost thou not judge and avenge our blood on them that dwell on the earth? (Rev.6:10)

The day of vengeance is the day of wrath of God, against the unbelievers, against His enemies, and to protect His children. It shall come to pass on the day when Jesus the Christ returns as the King of kings and Lord of lords. For it is the day of vengeance of God Almighty, and Christ will reign for a thousand years.

> **Which in his times he shall *shew*, *who is* the blessed and only Potentate, the King of kings, and Lord of lords;** (1Tim.6:15)
>
> **For he must reign, till he hath put all enemies under his feet.** (1Cor.15:25)
>
> **For it is written, *As* I live, saith the Lord, every knee shall bow to me, and every tongue shall confess to God.** (Rom.14:11)
>
> **So then every one of us shall give account of himself to God.** (Rom.14:12)

There is a significant and critical warning from Jesus Christ Himself to the unlearned of God's word, to those who are spiritually asleep or spiritually drunk, for they are confused about God's word, and to the spiritually blind for they are in darkness; they cannot see the truth. This warning is in the teaching of Jesus Christ from the "Parable of the Ten Virgins" (Matt.25:1–12). The five "foolish virgins" who are unlearned, end up being deceived and spiritually impregnated by the Antichrist (the first bridegroom that appears at midnight). The oil symbolizes God's truth, which cannot be purchased or bought. To acquire knowledge of God's truth, we must study, learn and absorb the truth from the word of God. Those five "foolish virgins" are good people, they do love the Lord, but unfortunately have been misled. They simply are unaware that they have been worshipping the Antichrist, just before the return of the true Christ for the day of vengeance of our God. The five "wise virgins" on the other hand, that have enough of God's truth, patiently waited for the real bridegroom, and they kept their spiritual virginity until the true Christ returned, ready to take part in the great marriage supper. Bear in mind that when God says something must happen, it surely will come to pass. For all prophecy will be fulfilled, just as it is written.

> **For these be the days of vengeance, that all things which are written may be fulfilled.** (Lk.21:22)
>
> **But woe unto them that are with child, and to them that give suck, in those days! for there shall be great distress in the land, and wrath upon this people.** (Lk.21:23)
>
> **For, behold, the days are coming, in the which they shall say, Blessed** *are* **the barren, and the wombs that never bare, and the paps which never gave suck.** (Lk.23:29)

No one knows when the day of vengeance of our God will come to pass, only heavenly Father the Almighty God. Remember that "thief" was one of Satan's many roles and names. Jesus said:

> **All that ever came before me are thieves and robbers ...** (John 10:8)

The thief cometh not, but for to steal, and to kill, and to destroy ... (John 10:10)

Know and understand that before Christ's return, the "thief" will come to steal people's crown of life, that is the eternal life — your salvation through Jesus Christ. Using lies and deception, the devil will spiritually destroy many. Destroying people's salvation will cause spiritual death, which is why Jesus taught and warned people about the "thief," urging people to be vigilant, watchful, spiritually awake, and prepared for the spiritual war before the end of this present world age:

> **But of that day and hour knoweth no *man*, no, not the angels of heaven, but my Father only.** (Matt.24:36)
>
> **Watch therefore: for ye know not what hour** (*daylight hour*) **your Lord doth come.** (Matt.24:42)
>
> **But know this, that if the goodman of the house had known in what watch** (*nighttime*) **the thief would come, he would have watched, and would not have suffered his house to be broken up.** (Matt.24:43)
>
> **Therefore be ye also ready: for in such an hour as ye think not the Son of man cometh.** (Matt.24:44)

Therefore, if people knew exactly when the "thief in the night" would break in to steal, then naturally they would stay awake for the thief's arrival. They would be on guard and be ready for him — defending their house against the thief's unwelcome visit.

In other words, if people know and understand enough of God's Word, then they're capable of identifying the false Christ — they knew that Satan the "thief" will appear on earth and claim that he the Christ. So being spiritually awake will enable to escape from the deception of the Antichrist, avoiding worship to the fake Christ. Jesus said: you also must be ready! Be mentally and spiritually ready — it will happen.

Be ready and prepare *before* the end of this world age. Because when Jesus Christ returns, whether we're ready or not, this present age of salvation will be over. It is the ending of this world age and the beginning of the millennial age.

There will be war in heaven, and this is time for Michael the archangel to throw down and release Satan onto this earth. When that happens, Satan walks on Earth for a short time. He will deceive a lot of people. Satan will come as the Antichrist, claiming that he is God, while many will be convinced that he is the Christ. After the Antichrist is exposed that he is a false Christ, the true Christ returns, as King of kings and Lord of lords, and many will be very surprised indeed.

> **And there was war in heaven: Michael and his angels fought against the dragon; and the dragon fought and his angels,** (Rev.12:7)
>
> **And prevailed not; neither was their place found any more in heaven.** (Rev.12:8)

And the great dragon was cast out, that old serpent, called the Devil, and Satan, which deceiveth the whole world: he was cast out into the earth, and his angels were cast out with him. (Rev.12:9).

Woe to the inhabiters of the earth and of the sea! for the devil is come down unto you, having great wrath, because he knoweth that he hath but a short time. (Rev.12:12).

Let us learn more about the "thief" from the teaching of the Apostle Paul. We will find it in his first letter to the Thessalonians. When Paul talks about the return of the Lord Jesus Christ to the Thessalonians, he said there's no need for him to explain the chronological order of events, because they knew it perfectly well that the day of the Lord comes like a thief in the night. For they fully understood the teaching of Jesus — referenced in the book of Matthew, chapter twenty-four. The Thessalonians also understood what must transpire first before the return of Jesus Christ. They knew that Christ's return will be as a "thief in the night." For those who are unlearned of God's word, for they are "foolish" as Jesus described them in the Parable of the Ten Virgins. For the foolish virgins it will be destruction instead of peace and safety. The foolish will be taken by surprise by the "thief," and unable to escape from the smooth deception of the Antichrist. They were ignorant of the "fake" Christ who will appear first, the Antichrist — aka the "thief in the night." The foolish were unaware that there is a false Christ and the true Christ. That is why Jesus also told the five foolish virgins, "I know you not" (Matt.25:12). That's exactly what Jesus warned: don't be deceived!

Let us listen and learn once again from Apostle Paul (1Thessalonians 5:1–8):

> **But of the times and the seasons, brethren, ye have no need that I write unto you.** (1Thess.5:1)
>
> **For yourselves know perfectly that the day of the Lord so cometh as a thief in the night.** (1Thess.5:2)
>
> **For when they shall say, Peace and safety; then sudden destruction cometh upon them, as travail upon a woman with child; and they shall not escape.** (1Thess.5:3)

So when the true Christ returns at the seventh trump, most will be surprised and terrified, realizing it was the "thief" all along and not Jesus the Christ who they have been devoted to. It will be sudden destruction indeed, for the unlearned of God's Word. Immediately after the true Christ's return emerges birth of a new age — the Millennium Year. Unfortunately, it will be a little too late for those who never had an opportunity to learn the truth, for they had already believed and worshipped the Antichrist — the devil.

Satan is the prince of darkness. Darkness is the absence of light, and it symbolizes spiritual blindness. The spiritually blind cannot see "truth," as it is hidden by darkness. Being spiritually blind means not having a clear understanding of God's Word, which is the "Light."

But those who are learned and well-informed in the word of God have the knowledge of the truth, and they are not in darkness — they are the "Children of Light." And Christ is that Light, that was "the light" of (Gen.1:3) — the Gospel is the light — the spiritual Hope of the world.

> **And God said, Let there be light: and there was light.** (Gen.1:3)
>
> **In him was life; and the life was the light of men.** (John 1:4)
>
> **And the light shineth in darkness; and the darkness comprehended it not.** (John 1:5)
>
> **But if our gospel be hid, it is hid to them that are lost:** (2Cor.4:3)

To those who cannot understand the gospel of Jesus Christ, the light is hidden to them because they will never understand the word of God.

> **In whom the god of this world hath blinded the minds of them which believe not, lest the light of the glorious gospel of Christ, who is the image of God, should shine unto them.** (2Cor.4:4)

The god of this world age is Satan, and his focus this time is, to blind the people's spiritual eyes from seeing the truth of God's Word, to prevent them from seeing the light of the glorious gospel of Jesus Christ.

However, the "children of light" can see truth, they have eyes to see, for they know and understand the word of God:

> **But ye, brethren, are not in darkness, that that day should overtake you as a thief. (1Thess.5:4)**
>
> **Ye are all the children of light, and the children of the day: we are not of the night, nor of darkness. (1Thess.5:5)**
>
> **Therefore let us not sleep, as *do* others; but let us watch and be sober. (1Thess.5:6)**
>
> **For they that sleep sleep in the night; and they that be drunken are drunken in the night. (1Thess.5:7)**
>
> **But let us, who are of the day, be sober, putting on the breastplate of faith and love; and for an helmet, the hope of salvation. (1Thess.5:8)**

Apostle Peter gave the same advice about the "thief," he also strongly encourage people to be spiritually awake, and to be watchful for any possible danger, from being destroyed through lies and deception by the adversary the devil:

> **The Lord is not slack concerning his promise, as some men count slackness; but is longsuffering to us-ward, not willing that any should perish, but that all should come to repentance. (2Peter 3:9)**
>
> **But the day of the Lord will come as a thief in the night; ... (2Peter 3:10)**

Be sober, be vigilant; because your adversary the devil, as a roaring lion, walketh about, seeking whom he may devour: (1Peter 5:8)

Therefore, watch and be ready for the spiritual war against Satan, because there will be struggle with the powers of evil. Study and learn the word of God to prepare our mind and spirit for what's going to happen before Jesus Christ's return, so that when it does happen, there won't be any surprises. You know how to overcome, and you'll know how to escape from the deception of the Antichrist.

As we see the importance of this prophecy concerning the second coming of Jesus Christ — "the day of vengeance of our God" (Isa.61:2). Paul did not want anyone to be deceived by the Antichrist, so he reminded the Thessalonians once again in his second letter, telling them not to allow anyone mislead them, believing that Christ had already returned. Because the return of the Lord Jesus Christ will not happen until apostasy takes place first, that is when Satan sets himself in the temple of God and declare that he himself is God. Many will fall into his deception, and many will abandon their previous beliefs and religions to worship this new-found god. Next will be the revealing of the man of sin — the son of perdition, which is Satan the Antichrist:

> Now we beseech you, brethren, by the coming of our Lord Jesus Christ, and *by* our gathering together unto him, (2Thess.2:1)
>
> That ye be not soon shaken in mind, or be troubled, neither by spirit, nor by word, nor by letter as from us, as that the day of Christ is at hand. (2Thess.2:2)
>
> Let no man deceive you by any means: for *that day shall not come*, except there come a falling away (*apostasy*) first, and that man of sin be revealed, the son of perdition; (2Thess.2:3)
>
> Who opposeth and exalteth himself above all that is called God, or that is worshipped; so that he as God sitteth in the temple of God, shewing himself that he is God. (2Thess.2:4)
>
> Remember ye not, that, when I was yet with you, I told you these things? (2Thess.2:5)

Unfortunately, as it is written, the Antichrist will deceive many; people will be spiritually blinded from seeing the truth. Many will believe the lies and worship the Antichrist, (certainly) not knowing he is actually the fake Christ.

> And all that dwell upon the earth shall worship him, whose names are not written in the book of life of the Lamb slain from the foundation of the world. (Rev.13:8)

Thankfully, Apostle Paul taught us how to avoid worshipping the Antichrist, to avoid being overtaken by the "thief," who wants to take our crown of life, and to avoid being destroyed by lies that will lead us right to spiritual death. Paul taught us how to prepare and to be ready for the spiritual war against Satan, and that is, to wear the whole Armor of God. We are going to need every piece of it to prevail. It is for defense and to protect our own crown of life (eternal life). When the devil appears on earth as the Antichrist, we will need all the Armor of God on, to stand against all the fiery darts of the devil, e.g. the deception, lies, accusation, evil tricks, etc. The war is not physical with flesh men, the war is spiritual war against Satan, against the rulers of darkness of this world age. No one would want to be part of those that are being deceived. So, let's listen and learn from the teaching of Paul to the Ephesians:

> **Put on the whole armour of God, that ye may be able to stand against the wiles** (*deceit, tricks*) **of the devil.** (Eph.6:11)
>
> **For we wrestle not against flesh and blood, but against principalities, against powers, against the rulers of the darkness of this world, against spiritual wickedness in high places.** (Eph.6:12)
>
> **Wherefore take unto you the whole armour of God, that ye may be able to withstand in the evil day, and having done all, to stand.** (Eph.6:13)

The "truth" of God's word is part of the Armor of God which we will need to prevail, and it will need an adequate understanding of God's Word to know the Truth, so that we will be able to fasten ourselves with the knowledge of the Truth. We will need "righteousness," and that righteousness is what people earned and accumulated by doing things God's way, by doing what is right and what is pleasing to Almighty God. We also need to be prepared and ready to share the good news of everlasting peace; that is, the Lord and Savior Jesus Christ.

> **Stand therefore, having your loins girt about with truth, and having on the breastplate of righteousness;** (Eph.6:14)
>
> **And your feet shod with the preparation of the gospel of peace;** (Eph.6:15)

The most important of all about the armor of God is "faith." Make sure that we have faith in Jesus Christ. If we know Jesus Christ thoroughly well, we cannot help but to trust Him. Having faith, loving and trusting Jesus the Christ requires no effort at all, if we have the true knowledge of God the Father, e.g. knowing His infinite wisdom, His love, His will and His overall plan for His children There's only one way to know our Heavenly Father — God Almighty has revealed Himself to us through His written Word, through His only begotten Son Jesus the Christ — the living Word, so that we may know and understand the invisible God, the Creator of all things.

Our faith in the Lord and Savior Jesus Christ is what we need the most, to survive in the spiritual war. We will need the defender — "the shield of faith" which is to say Jesus Christ. He will deflect and protect anyone from all the fiery darts of the wicked, but it will depend on how strong our faith is in Jesus Christ. Know that He is with you, so there is nothing to fear. Know that through the Holy

Spirit, He is going to save you and protect you, and know that He will never forsake you. By faith we receive the "helmet of salvation" for defense, and the Holy Spirit as the sword, that is, the "word of God" — the Truth, and truth will always prevail.

> **Above all, taking the shield of faith, wherewith ye shall be able to quench all the fiery darts of the wicked.** (Eph.6:16)
>
> **And take the helmet of salvation, and the sword of the Spirit, which is the word of God:** (Eph.6:17)

The word of God is "sharper than any two-edged sword" (Heb.4:12). To know and understand the word of God will make anyone perfectly capable of distinguishing true from false. Having the word of God in our hearts and minds, and most importantly, through the help of the Holy Spirit, we will prevail in the spiritual war against Satan and will not suffer spiritual death. Therefore, patiently wait for the true Christ to come, don't allow the "fake," the "thief" to steal your crown of life.

> **Finally, my brethren, be strong in the Lord, and in the power of his might.** (Eph.6:10)

We will need God's strength to be an overcomer; we will need that power from God to overcome the temptation; we need to be clothed with the whole armor of God, and we need Christ's protection against the rulers of this world. God's strength is the only power that will allow us to stand against the deception of the Antichrist, so stay focused on God's word. With the whole armor of God in place, you can overcome the Antichrist with the power of God.

For God's elect — those that were chosen before the foundation of the world (Eph.1:4), the "sword" will be given unto them by the Holy Spirit, at the right time, for a testimony. So that the whole world can hear the truth, a testimony for the Lord Jesus Christ — the Holy Spirit will speak through God's elect:

> **But take heed to yourselves: for they shall deliver you up to councils; and in the synagogues ye shall be beaten: and ye shall be brought before rulers and kings for my sake, for a testimony against them.** (Mk.13:9)
>
> **And the gospel must first be published among all nations.** (Mk.13:10)
>
> **But when they shall lead** *you*, **and deliver you up, take no thought beforehand what ye shall speak, neither do ye premeditate: but whatsoever shall be given you in that hour, that speak ye: for it is not ye that speak, but the Holy Ghost.** (Mk.13:11)

Let us bear in mind the word of Jesus when He was asked privately by His disciples, concerning His second coming and the end of this world age. Jesus Christ warned to beware that no one misleads you before His return, because many will come in His name, claiming to be Christian, claiming to be the Christ, and they will mislead

The Day of Vengeance

many. It's important to recognize and understand "the abomination of desolation," which is the coming of the desolator, that is Satan himself, the false Messiah spoken of by the prophet Daniel (Dan.9:27):

> And as he sat upon the mount of Olives over against the temple, Peter and James and John and Andrew asked him privately, (Mk.13:3)
>
> Tell us, when shall these things be? and what *shall be* the sign when all these things shall be fulfilled? (Mk.13:4)
>
> And Jesus answering them began to say, Take heed lest any *man* deceive you: (Mk.13:5)
>
> For many shall come in my name, saying, I am *Christ*; and shall deceive many. (Mk.13:6)
>
> But when ye shall see the abomination of desolation, spoken of by Daniel the prophet, standing where it (*he*) ought not, (let him that readeth understand,) then let them that be in Judaea flee to the mountains: (Mk.13:14)
>
> For *in* those days shall be affliction, such as was not from the beginning of the creation which God created unto this time, neither shall be. (Mk.13:19)
>
> And except that the Lord had shortened those days, no flesh should be saved: but for the elect's sake, whom he hath chosen, he hath shortened the days. (Mk.13:20)

For the sake of God's elect, those days will be cut short. The Lord shortened those days to five months, instead of three and a half years. Therefore, Satan will only have five months to deceive the people on earth:

> And they had tails like unto scorpions, and there were stings in their tails: and their power *was* to hurt men five months. (Rev.9:10)
>
> And they had a king over them, *which is* the angel of the bottomless pit, whose name in the Hebrew tongue *is* Abaddon, but in the Greek tongue hath *his* name Apollyon. (Rev.9:11).

The false Christ will appear and will perform miracles, and many will believe and will worship the false Christ, without knowing it is the Antichrist. That is why when they tell you that Christ has returned, Jesus said, do not believe it, because it is the FAKE.

> And then if any man shall say to you, Lo, here *is* Christ; or, lo, *he is* there; believe *him* not: (Mk.13:21)
>
> For false Christs and false prophets shall rise, and shall shew signs and wonders, to seduce, if *it were* possible, even the elect. (Mk.13:22)
>
> But take ye heed: behold, I have foretold you all things. (Mk.13:23)

Jesus Christ foretold us all things, so that we can avoid being misled by those that will claim to be of Christ. These signs and wonders will not be just tricks of illusion, but it will be supernatural, and because of these miracles, many people will be convinced, and will think it is Jesus Christ indeed. That is why many will be deceived by the Antichrist. So, let us be familiar with the gospel armor of God.

As we have learned the *"katabole"* (the foundation of the world) from chapter one, there were some of God's children who decided to join Satan and turn against God from the first earth age. So, there is an irreconcilable difference between God and Satan; there is an enmity between God and Satan, and that is the reason for the spiritual war.

However, there were also few that were chosen by God (the elect) before the overthrow of Satan, because they stood with God during Satan's rebellion against God. They did not believe the lies and deception of Satan in the first earth age, and they still are not going to in this present earth age when Satan will play his role as the Antichrist. Because "the elect" already had a destiny and a purpose — the destiny according to the will of God (God's plan), and the purpose to save the lost souls. God Almighty selects His chosen people to accomplish His overall plan.

> **According as he hath chosen us in him before the foundation of the world, that we should be holy and without blame before him in love:** (Eph.1:4)
>
> **Having predestinated us unto the adoption of children by Jesus Christ to himself, according to the good pleasure of his will,** (Eph.1:5)

> **In whom also we have obtained an inheritance, being predestinated according to the purpose of him who worketh all things after the counsel of his own will:** (Eph.1:11)

God Almighty, the Creator of all things, fathered all His children through creation. God created all the souls in the first earth and heaven age, God gave them the freedom of choice, and the freedom to decide for themselves, so God the Father knew what good or bad that every soul did from the first earth and heaven age. We have good example; like Jeremiah, Jacob and Esau, before they were born in this present earth age, God said to Jeremiah the prophet;

> **Before I formed thee in the belly, I knew thee; and before thou camest forth out of the womb I sanctified thee, *and* I ordained thee a prophet unto the nations.** (Jer.1:5)

God knew He can trust, and He can use Jeremiah, because of the choices he made and the things that he decided to do in the first earth age, and that, pleases the heavenly Father. So, he was chosen to be a prophet in this present world age.

To Jacob that did good, and to Esau that did bad; while they were both still in their mother's womb, God said,

"**... Jacob have I loved, but Esau have I hated.**" (Rom.9:13)

In this present earth age, God also gave all His children the freedom of choice, and the freedom to decide for themselves, and

God allows all His children to be tested. Whosoever endure the temptation of antichrist, will gain the "crown of life," that is, the eternal life through the Lord Jesus Christ into the eternity.

The way to escape or to endure the temptation is to know and understand the word of God, to put on the whole armor of God.

Our Heavenly Father is very patient, and not willing for any of His children should perish, but all would need to know the truth, and come to repentance — to have eternal life, and to be with Him in eternity.

> **Blessed *is* the man that endureth temptation: for when he is tried, he shall receive the crown of life, which the Lord hath promised to them that love him.** (James 1:12)
>
> **Because thou hast kept the word of my patience, I also will keep thee from the hour of temptation, which shall come upon all the world, to try them that dwell upon the earth.** (Rev.3:10)
>
> **Behold, I come quickly: hold that fast which thou hast, that no man take thy crown.** (Rev.3:11)

In this present earth age, God has given everybody free will (except "the elect"), the freedom to decide for ourselves: whether we want to be ready or not for the spiritual war, whether we want to become familiar or not with the Gospel Armor of God, to be clothed or not to be clothed in the gospel armor — we decide, it's our choice.

Heavenly Father wants to give all His children the opportunity to make that decision and find salvation, when the devil appears on earth as the Antichrist. Because we are going to need the whole armor of God; we are going to need Jesus Christ's protection. Without the power from God, there is no way we can withstand all the fiery darts of Satan.

Just like the saints at Ephesus, they made a choice and decided to believe after hearing the word of God and the gospel of salvation from apostle Paul:

> **That we** (*God's elect*) **should be to the praise of his glory, who first trusted in Christ.** (Eph.1:12)
>
> **In whom ye** (*not elected, but willingly*) **also *trusted*, after that ye heard the word of truth, the gospel of your salvation: in whom also after that ye believed, ye were sealed with that holy Spirit of promise,** (Eph.1:13)

Heavenly Father loves all His children. That is the reason why, when God gave one of His children the "truth," He will require and expect them to share it to His other children that are lost in this world of darkness, including those who opposed the Father, who are enemies of God, for they are still God's children. God the Father wants to give His lost children an opportunity to be found, so that they may also find salvation in this present earth age — the Age of Salvation. Sometimes when God's children share the truth with others, they get opposition coming against them from the enemies of God, so God's enemy is also their enemy. That is why when Jesus was teaching His disciples privately, before they were sent out to teach the word of God to share the good news, the gospel of personal salvation. Jesus said: "love your enemies."

> **Ye have heard that it hath been said, Thou shalt love thy neighbour, and hate thine enemy.** (Matt.5:43)
>
> **But I say unto you, Love your enemies, bless them that curse you, do good to them that hate you, and pray for them which despitefully use you, and persecute you;** (Matt.5:44)
>
> **That ye may be the children of your Father which is in heaven: for he maketh his sun to rise on the evil and on the good, and sendeth rain on the just and on the unjust.** (Matt.5:45)

To love your enemy is to have compassion for them. If (only IF) they ask, and sincerely want to know the word of God, then share the truth. Share the gospel of salvation to them, so that they may have the opportunity to find eternal life also. You do not want them to perish, because you love them.

People should be concerned about "the day of vengeance of our God" (Isa. 61:2). Be concerned of how to obtain salvation through our Lord and Savior Jesus Christ: How to be more familiar with the word of God, how to accumulate enough truth that we can be mentally and spiritually ready for the spiritual war, and how to be spiritually prepared and awake to know who and what to watch out for. As Paul clearly taught:

> **Dearly beloved, avenge not yourselves, but *rather* give place unto wrath: for it is written, Vengeance *is* mine; I will repay, saith the Lord. (Rom.12:19)**
>
> **For God hath not appointed us to wrath, but to obtain salvation by our Lord Jesus Christ, (1Thess.5:9)**
>
> **Wherefore, my beloved, as ye have always obeyed, not as in my presence only, but now much more in my absence, work out your own salvation with fear and trembling. (Phil.2:12)**
>
> **For we know him that hath said, Vengeance *belongeth* unto me, I will recompense, saith the Lord. And again, The Lord shall judge his people. (Heb.10:30)**
>
> ***It is* a fearful thing to fall into the hands of the living God. (Heb.10:31)**

It is very fearful indeed, because only God Almighty can destroy our soul. That is the second death, which is the death of the soul and the spiritual body:

> **And fear not them which kill the body, but are not able to kill the soul: but rather fear him which is able to destroy both soul and body in hell. (Matt.10:28)**

Our heavenly Father has a book of life, and only He can blot out names from that book. On the final judgment, those that are still not qualified to participate in the second resurrection, their name will be blotted out from the book of life.

> **And whosoever was not found written in the book of life was cast into the lake of fire.** (Rev.20:15)

All of our record is in the book of life. The good deeds and the bad deeds are all recorded in there. Only God can blot out what is in that book, and when God blots it out, it is gone forever.

If we want to erase our bad deeds from the book of life, it requires action on our part. This is called repentance. Christ already accomplished His part on the cross. Therefore, with sincere repentance and asking our heavenly Father for forgiveness in Jesus' name, sins that we committed are blotted out from the book of life. So on judgment day we don't have to answer for it.

> **For by grace are ye saved through faith; and that not of yourselves:** *it is* **the gift of God:** (Eph.2:8)

> **Repent ye therefore, and be converted, that your sins may be blotted out, when the times of refreshing shall come from the presence of the Lord;** (Acts 3:19)

Therefore, let us put on the whole armor of God, let us overcome the temptation, let us overcome the deception of the Antichrist in this spiritual war. Through faith in the Lord Jesus Christ we can be an overcomer, and our name will be in the book of life, and we will be resurrected to eternal life.

He that hath an ear, let him hear what the Spirit saith unto the churches; He that overcometh shall not be hurt of the second death. (Rev.2:11).

He that overcometh, the same shall be clothed in white raiment; and I will not blot out his name out of the book of life, but I will confess his name before my Father, and before his angels. (Rev.3:5)

The grace of our Lord Jesus Christ *be* with you all. Amen.

www.ingramcontent.com/pod-product-compliance
Lightning Source LLC
Chambersburg PA
CBHW020937090426
42736CB00010B/1167